# DEDICATION

*To Ernie Price: my dad, my hero*

# DREAM MAKING IN A DREAM-TAKING WORLD

## 10 SUREFIRE STRATEGIES TO OVERCOME OBSTACLES AND LIVE YOUR DREAMS

DR. STEVE PRICE

Published by:

PENTAGON PRESS

Marketed by:

MANJUL

Manjul Publishing House

First published in India by:

**Pentagon Press,**
206, Peacock Lane,
Shahpur Jat, New Delhi, INDIA - 110 049

Exclusively distributed in India by:
**SV Book Supply Company Pvt. Ltd.**
7 / 32, Ground floor, Ansari Road, Daryaganj, New Delhi - 110 002
Email: booksupplyco@gmail.com

***Dream Making in a Dream-Taking World***
*10 Surefire Strategies to Overcome Obstacles and Live Your Dreams*
*by Dr. Steve Price*



This edition first published in 2012

**ISBN 978-81-8274-579-7**

Cover design by Alane Bearder
Text layout by Parry Design Studio
Cover photography © Thinkstock; Photodisk

Printed & bound in India by Manipal Technologies Ltd., Manipal.

# ACKNOWLEDGMENT

How do I, someone who has lived more than half a century, begin to acknowledge all of the people who've had a hand in shaping me, and, in so doing, have contributed to this book?

Here goes my best effort:

Special thanks to my creative team: Burke Hedges for motivating me to write and mentoring me to improve; Katherine Glover for balancing the tightrope between cheerleader and critic; and Bill Quain for helping me turn so-so ideas into really good ones.

"What-would-I-do-without-you?" to the INTI Publishing team: Sandee Lorenzen for cheerfully doing double duty as a cherished friend and invaluable assistant; Dee Garrand for smilingly doing great work on short notice; Gail Brown for putting the Humpty-Dumpty of our accounting department back together again; and Julia Bullough for being versatile enough to do five different things and all of them well.

"I-love-you-to-pieces" to my lifelong friends: Greg Harris, my best friend and counselor on-call; Luke and Patti Gleason, who laugh at my jokes but never at my blunders; Derrel Davis for reminding me that people who grow up in dysfunctional families are better off focusing on the *fun*-part of the family than the *dys*-part; Jeff and Marti Wilday for reminding me that the real cash crop of Illinois isn't soybeans and corn, but solid values and community; Wes and Charlotte Brown for being part-parents and all-friends for 30-plus years; Al Taylor for sharing a thousand laughs over hundreds of pizzas, starting our sophomore year in college; Dave and Terri Neff and Dick and Linda Rakers for proving that "living happily ever after" happens outside of fairy tales; Jim Wyeth, my high school coach, for letting me think he was teaching me the game of tennis when he was really teaching me the game of life; Carol Edler for showing me that talking is more fun than television, any day; Charmaine Smith for teaching me that true friendship is more about acceptance than understanding; Tim and Kathleen Shears for reminding me that we have to make time for our friends before we run out of time; Barb Bitschenhauer, Jeff Keller, the Honeyman women, Claire Raines, Jill Cook, and Wes Coulter for nudging me gently in the direction of my dreams; and last but not least, my 1982 first-hour English class for teaching me about the beauty of relationships while I was trying to teach them about the beauty of language and literature.

"I-wouldn't-trade-you-for-a-million-dollars" to my daughter, Sydney, whose birth immediately inspired me to place unconditional love on the top rung of my ladder of values.

And finally, to all the dreamers, past and present, who had the stamina and courage to become Dream Makers in a dream-taking world. This is your book. These are your stories. May they inspire others to set aside their doubts and pursue their dreams.

# Dreaming Is Like Oxygen—You Can't Live Without It!

*I'm a big fan of dreams. Unfortunately, dreams are our first casualty in life. People seem to give them up, quicker than anything, for a "reality."*

–Kevin Costner,
Academy Award winning actor and director

What's the big deal about dreaming?

That's like asking, "What's the big deal about oxygen?" Fact is, we need both of them to live!

That's why there are so many books about dreaming. Last time I checked, Amazon.com listed 4,657 books with the word "dream" in the title. Wow! That's a lot of books on the same topic!

So, why do I think the world needs another dream book? One simple reason—most dream books do a great job of telling us about the power of dreaming. But they fail to tell us what to do when things don't go according to plan. So, we naively follow the books' advice: We dream big dreams. We make our dream list. We tape a photo of our dream house on the refrigerator. And we march out the front door to make our dreams come true. Then, suddenly, without warning—BLAM!!!—*we run headfirst into reality!*

## Reality Check!

*Reality check:* Friends tell us to get our head out of the clouds and quit dreaming.

*Reality check:* People won't return our phone calls.

*Reality check:* We're overworked and underpaid, but the bills still keep coming in!

*Reality check:* The hot water heater springs a leak in the middle of the night, and the plumber is on vacation.

You get the idea.

Here's my point: All the dream books I've read conveniently ignore the fact that we live in a dream-taking world. As a result, the first time adversity strikes (and rest assured, it *will* strike in one form or another), we get blown out of the water! When our dreams are suddenly confronted with a dream-taking world, we don't know what to do. So, most of us slink back into the house, grab a shovel, head to the back yard, and bury our dreams.

So sad. And *so* unnecessary!

## Dream Making in a Dream-Taking World

I believe that most people have bought into a myth about successful people. Most people think that successful people—I call them "Dream Makers"—have fewer challenges than the rest of us, which is the reason Dream Makers get to live their dreams while we have to "settle for living in the real world."

But as you'll soon discover in this book, that's just a myth.

Here's the truth. Dream Makers don't live in a trouble-free parallel universe. They live and work side by side with us in the same dream-taking world. Which means *we all* face challenges—big, small, and everything in between. Truth is, Dream Makers don't live their dreams because they have an *absence of challenges in their lives.* Dream Makers live their dreams because *they have an abundance of strategies* that enable them to overcome their challenges.

## Learn Their Strategies, Live Your Dreams!

That's why I titled this book, *Dream Making in a Dream-Taking World.* I wanted to remind you that life isn't always fair. That bad things happen to good people. *But that you can still live your dreams!* How? By learning and practicing the 10 proven dream-making strategies in this book.

Look, if you aren't living your dreams, it's *not* because your dreams are too big.

And it's certainly *not* because your talent is too small.

If you aren't living your dreams, it's because you aren't practicing the right Dream Making strategies. When all is said and done, the key to becoming a Dream Maker is simple:

First you *learn their strategies.*

Then you *live your dreams!*

# CONTENTS

CONTENTS

INTRODUCTION



# 10 SUPERIOR STRATEGIES TO OVERCOME OBSTACLES AND LIVE YOUR DREAMS



CONCLUSION

INTRODUCTION

# DREAM MAKING IN A DREAM-TAKING WORLD

*I'll drive the truck,*
*If you'll fight the fire.*
*I'll plunk the keys,*
*If you'll be the choir.*
*I'll find the ball,*
*If you'll call the team.*
*Let's put our heads together,*
*And dream the same dream.*

From the poem "Together"
by George Ellen Lyon

INTRODUCTION

# Dream Making in a Dream-Taking World

*Nothing is as real as a dream. The world can change around you, but your dream will not. Responsibilities need not erase it. Duties need not obscure it. Because the dream is within you, no one can take it away.*

–Tom Clancy,
bestselling author

Poor little Dave started life with two strikes against him.

Strike one happened when Dave's birth mother gave him up for adoption.

Strike two occurred five years later when his adoptive mother died, leaving Dave to be raised by a cold, distant father.

To complicate matters, Dave's father moved from state to state looking for work, which meant Dave seldom spent more than a few months in the same school. Not surprisingly, Dave was never much of a student, and he seemingly sealed his fate to a life of failure when he quit high school at 15 and moved out to live on his own.

Poor Dave. No mother. Cold father. High school dropout. The prisons are full of angry, poorly educated men who, like Dave, suffered through unstable, loveless childhoods.

But instead of ending up with his photo on a prison mug shot, Dave ended up with his photo on the cover of *Fortune* magazine. That's because Dave was none other than Dave Thomas, founder and CEO of the Wendy's hamburger chain.

## The Power of a Dream

Why was it that Dave Thomas was able to overcome a traumatic childhood to become one of the greatest success stories of the 20th century?

The answer—*Dave had a dream!*

You see, when Dave was growing up, he and his father ate out almost every night. The only place where Dave ever felt the warmth of family life was when he sat next to families at restaurants. So, by age 12, Dave decided he'd own his own restaurant some day. Fueled by that dream, Dave worked in restaurants until age 26, when he met an eccentric-looking senior citizen wearing a cream-colored white suit with a black string tie. It was Colonel Sanders, founder of Kentucky Fried Chicken.

Before long, Dave took over four failing KFC restaurants in Columbus, Ohio, revived them, and sold them back to KFC for $1.5 million. Dave was 35 and a millionaire!

But instead of retiring, Dave set about pursuing his dream with a passion. In 1969, he opened his first Wendy's. When Dave passed away 33 years later at age 69, Wendy's had grown to 6,000 restaurants in dozens of countries.

Dave Thomas—business icon... family man with a wife of 47 years, six children, and 15 grandchildren... a philanthropist who started and donated millions to the Dave Thomas Center for Adoption—is testimony to *the power of a dream!*

## Dream Making in a Dream-Taking World

If Dave Thomas were the only person to overcome huge obstacles to become a mega-success, we could say that dreaming was a waste of time. But the truth is, there are thousands, if not millions, of Dave Thomas-type success stories... stories of people's dreams spurring them on to triumph in the face of adversity. I call these people "Dream Makers," for they make their dreams come true despite hardships and setbacks in their lives.

That's why I titled this book, *Dream Making in a Dream-Taking World!* Because that's what Dream Makers, such as Dave Thomas, do—they find a way to overcome obstacles and make their dreams come true. Dream Makers recognize that life isn't fair. That bad things happen to good people. That we live in a dream-taking world. But that doesn't stop Dream Makers from living their dreams. Dream Makers face their challenges head on and do what needs to be done to turn their dreams into reality.

Dream Makers deal with real challenges and solve real problems just like real adults do. Instead of using hardships and setbacks to make excuses, Dream Makers use the strategies outlined in this book to make dreams come true!

## What Dreaming Has Meant to My Life

I didn't really begin to understand the power of dreaming until 1991. Yes, I suppose I'd had dreams in my life before then. When I was 10, I dreamed of being a professional baseball player. But in my heart of hearts, I knew that was more a fantasy than a dream.

But until 1991, I didn't think about the choices I made in my life in terms of dreams. Up to then, the concept of dreaming just wasn't part of my self-talk. One phone conversation with an old college buddy, Luke Gleason, changed all that. Here's my story:

Upon graduating from college in 1968, I took a job as an English teacher at Southeast High School in Springfield, Illinois. I was 22 years old, full of optimism, and passionate about my job. But gradually over the years, the realities of teaching teenagers eroded my enthusiasm. I spent the biggest part of my day settling petty squabbles and trying to convince 15-year-olds that I knew what I was talking about. It got to the point where I didn't like my job and didn't like myself. With each advancing year, I became more and more disillusioned with teaching. It was time for a change, but I didn't know what else to go into.

## Opportunity Knocks Twice!

Then in 1982, after 14 years of teaching, I received two pieces of mail that dramatically altered the direction of my life. The first was a letter from Illinois State University promoting a new doctoral program in English Composition. I stopped dead in my tracks when I read that letter:

*"Wouldn't it be great to go back to school and get a doctorate?"* I thought to myself. *"Maybe that would open up some doors for me."*

One problem—ISU was an hour and a half away, and it would take me at least 10 years to complete my doctorate commuting to ISU and taking one course each semester. My stomach knotted up at the thought of managing a classroom of complaining teenagers for 10 more years....

The second piece of mail arrived several months later. It was a letter from the school board announcing a program to award a paid sabbatical to a teacher to further their education.

*"This is my ticket out!"* I thought to myself. *"I can finish at least half my doctorate in a year. I've got to get this paid sabbatical!"*

The school district had more than 2,500 teachers and administrators, so I knew I wouldn't be the only person to apply. I didn't like my odds of getting the sabbatical, so I set about stacking the odds in my favor. I arranged for a friend to introduce me to the administrator who headed up the sabbatical committee. When I found out he taught an evening class at the local university, I enrolled in his class. I made it a point to talk with him after each session. I wrote two letters to him explaining why I would be the best candidate for the sabbatical and how my students would benefit from my course of study.

*I got the sabbatical!*

## Florida, or Bust!

The sabbatical enabled me to fast-track my studies, and in 1985, I was awarded my doctorate. The next year I resigned from teaching, loaded all my belongings into a dented up U-Haul, and headed to Tampa, Florida.

I had $20,000 in savings, owned a 12-year-old Mercedes diesel that belched smoke, and owed $2,000 in credit card debt. I had no job and no place to live. I figured I could live for two years off my savings until I got a business going. I was 40 years old, full of hope, and free to chart my own course in life.

For the first four years in Tampa, I tried five different businesses. Four failed miserably. But one turned out great! I hooked up with a young entrepreneur who had developed a sales training program. His ideas were great. But the writing needed polishing. I persuaded the young entrepreneur to hire me for $2,000 a month for three months to write, edit, and market materials for him. If he liked my work, he'd hire me full time. If not, we'd go our separate ways, no questions asked. In the fall of 1990, we shook hands on the deal. We've been partners ever since.

You may have heard of my partner, by the way. His name is Burke Hedges. During the last 11 years, Burke and I have worked on seven books together. Good chance you've read one or more of his books: *Who Stole the American Dream?*... *You Can't Steal Second with Your Foot on First!*... *You, Inc*.... *Copycat Marketing 101*... *Read & Grow Rich*... *Dream-Biz.com*... and *Parable of the Pipeline*. With book sales totaling more than 3 million copies and translations into 20 different languages, I'd say our three-month trial period has worked out nicely for both of us!

## What, Me Dream?

It was shortly after inking my partnership with Burke that I got the telephone call from my old college buddy, Luke. I told him about my new partnership. I told him about the three apartment buildings I owned. I told him how much I loved Tampa and how delighted I was to have resigned from teaching five years earlier. And I'll never forget his response:

*"Steve, you had a dream, and now you're living it,"* Luke said. As I recall, I laughed at his remark, made some wisecrack, and changed the subject. "Me, living a dream?" I thought to myself. "That's for movie stars and pro athletes and millionaire CEOs. I'm just a regular guy trying to get by."

Sure, I was enjoying more success than I ever had imagined. I owned my own business. Worked with talented authors. Published books that helped people grow themselves and their businesses. But I'd never thought of my life in terms of "living a dream." The concept of dreaming just wasn't part of my self-talk until Luke put a name to it. But once I heard the word "dream," I couldn't get it out of my mind:

"Me, a dreamer?" I'd say to myself. "Do dreams *really* have the power to shape futures? Can anyone make their dreams come true?"

> Nothing happens unless first a dream.
>
> –Carl Sandburg, American poet

At first, the concept of dreaming sounded awfully soft and fuzzy to a practical guy like me. But the more I thought about dreams... and the more I read and talked about dreams with Burke... the more I realized that dreams weren't just passing fancies that never came true.

If reality is *who we are* right now, right this moment, then *dreams are the blueprints for what we become.* That's not a passing fancy. That's not soft and fuzzy. That's just the truth! Best of all, I realized that dreams aren't reserved just for actors and athletes. *Dreams are for everyone!*

## Strategies for Turning Dreams into Reality

Over the years, I've made it a personal mission to become a student of dreaming. I've researched the lives of hundreds of successful people in dozens of endeavors: business... sports... entertainment... politics... medicine... charity... and education... to name a few. I've interviewed dozens of millionaires and professionals, as well as scores of "free spirits" who quit their jobs to pursue their dreams of making their living as painters, writers, musicians, and sculptors. Without exception, every one of these successful people had to overcome numerous hardships and setbacks on their way to living their dreams. That's why I call successful people "Dream Makers"—they start with a dream and then MAKE it happen!

As I researched Dream Makers, one question kept popping up in my mind: Why is it that the Dream Makers manage to rise above hardships and live their dreams, while so many others abandon their dreams in the face of adversity?

According to my research, the common thread that runs through the lives of all Dream Makers is this: Dream Makers don't live their dreams because they have *an absence of challenges.* Dream Makers live their dreams because *they have an abundance of strategies* that empower them to overcome their challenges!

It stands to reason that if people learn and practice these strategies, then they, too, can become Dream Makers.

## Dream Makers Dream... and then DO!

Let's not sugar coat it—everybody wants what Dream Makers ***have.*** But very few people ***do*** what Dream Makers ***do.*** Why? Well, for one thing, what Dream Makers *do* involves work and sacrifice and discipline. And let's face it, all too many people just aren't willing to do what it takes to make their dreams come true.

But I truly believe that most people would be willing to do what Dream Makers do, but most people are clueless as to what that is and how to begin. Well, that's no longer the case. I wrote this book to teach people what it is that Dream Makers do to turn their dreams into reality.

I've identified 10 strategies that successful people follow in order to become Dream Makers in a dream-taking world. I call them "10 Surefire Strategies to Overcome Obstacles and Live Your Dreams."

These 10 strategies are time-tested and proven. They work in Old Economy businesses, as well as New Economy businesses. They work for young people and old people... for men and women... for rich people and poor people... and for whites and blacks and Hispanics and Asians and every other ethnic group that ever walked the face of the earth.

Dave Thomas intuitively understood and practiced these strategies. So did dozens of other Dream Makers profiled in this book. Learn and practice the 10 strategies to overcome obstacles discussed in this book, and you, *too, can become a Dream Maker in a dream-taking world!*

# 10 Surefire Strategies to Overcome Obstacles and Live Your Dreams

*Since it doesn't cost a dime to dream, you'll never shortchange yourself when you stretch your imagination.*

–Dr. Robert Schuller,
minister and bestselling author

# STRATEGY 1

## Push the Envelope of Your Expectations

*America didn't invent dreaming. But it was the first to make dreaming available to the masses.*

–from a commercial honoring Walt Disney's 100th birthday

Fifty-seven cents and a dream—that's all it took to build an historic church and a major university.

Impossible, you say? Not only possible, but true.

Here's the rest of an amazing story:

In 1886, 8-year-old Hattie May Wiatt stood on the steps of a crowded Sunday school building in Philadelphia. Seeing that the frail, little girl would never be able to push her way inside, the pastor, Russell H. Conwell, lifted Hattie onto his shoulder and carried her through the crowd.

*"We need a bigger Sunday school,"* the little girl remarked as the kindly minister placed her in an empty seat.

*"Yes, we do,"* Conwell laughingly replied. *"And God willing, we will build one."*

Several days later, Conwell received a message that Hattie May was ill. He visited her home and prayed with her parents, but in his heart, he knew the end was near. Late that night he received the message he dreaded—Hattie May Wiatt had died. After the funeral, Hattie May's mother approached Conwell and handed him a small coin purse.

"Hattie wanted you to have this," she said through her tears. "She was saving it to help build a new Sunday school." Conwell emptied the contents into his hand. He counted 57 cents in pennies.

That Sunday the congregation was surprised to see a small coin purse sitting on the pulpit. Conwell told the story of unselfish devotion and sacrifice of the little girl who saved her pennies to build a new Sunday school. He challenged the congregation to raise the money by buying each one of Hattie's 57 pennies. By the next Sunday, Conwell had received $250 in donations for the pennies, enough to buy the house adjacent to the church property. Plus, 54 of Hattie's 57 pennies were returned to Conwell.

> It's all about dreams.
>
> –Tony Bennett, singer

The story of Hattie May's 57 cents traveled far and wide. Donations poured in from around the country. A wealthy businessman who owned several acres adjoining the sanctuary offered to sell his property to the church for far less than the market value. All he wanted for a down payment was Hattie's coin purse containing the remaining 54 pennies. The church now owned enough property for a major expansion.

Hattie's 57-cent donation may have inspired Conwell to dream, but over the years, he expanded his dream far beyond a bigger Sunday school. Not only was the Sunday school enlarged, but the small, wooden church was replaced by a magnificent 3,300-seat Temple Church. In the small house that was purchased with the $250 raised by selling

Hattie's 57 cents, Conwell organized Temple University, which quickly grew to surround Temple Church in downtown Philadelphia. In addition, Conwell oversaw the building of the Good Samaritan Hospital, now Temple University Hospital, on church property.

Today, Temple University is the country's eighth largest university, enrolling 35,000 students on five campuses, and Samaritan Hospital, renamed Temple University Hospital, treats 30,000 patients a year. Over the past 100-plus years, literally hundreds of thousands of lives have been touched by an eight-year-old girl's donation and a kindly minister's devotion. *And to think it all started with 57 cents... and a dream!*

## What Is Dreaming and Why Is It So Powerful?

The story of Hattie May Wiatt and Russell H. Conwell is a testimony to the power of dreaming. Just think—a new Sunday school... a new sanctuary... a hospital... and a major university had their beginnings in a few small coins and lots of big dreams. You see, Conwell recognized the fact that he lived in a dream-taking world, but he didn't let that prevent him from becoming a Dream Maker. He used every resource available to make his dreams come true—and they did!

So, what is a dream?... and why are dreams so powerful that they can transform 57 cents into dozens of buildings on the campus of a major university? Let's start by defining the word *dream*.

I define a dream as *"the process of pushing the envelope of your expectations."* The phrase "pushing the envelope" was coined by aircraft test pilots to describe the routines they put new aircraft through. The word "envelope" was test-pilot slang for the airplane. When the pilots "pushed the envelope," they flew the aircraft faster and higher than the manufacturer's specifications. By pushing the envelope, the pilots discovered the aircraft's ultimate potential—and more often than not, that potential exceeded the original expectations.

In effect, when we dream, we do the same thing test pilots do—we force ourselves to push beyond our own and other people's expectations, and we expand our vision of what we can become... do... have... and achieve.

## Believe in Your Dream and the Facts Don't Count

To paint a word picture, *a dream is a mental movie that begins with WHAT IS... and ends with WHAT COULD BE.* In Conwell's case, the reality of WHAT IS was a small church with very little money. But Conwell didn't choose to focus on the reality of the present. He chose to focus on the possibility of WHAT COULD BE in the future. In other words, Conwell kept pushing the envelope of his expectations.

Instead of turning kids away from the Sunday school, Conwell dreamed, "Let's build a bigger Sunday school building!"

Instead of settling for a small, wooden sanctuary, Conwell dreamed, "Why not build a big stone sanctuary?"

Instead of resigning himself to teaching a few would-be ministers in a drafty old house, Conwell dreamed, "Why not build a university to train thousands of seminary students?"

Do you see how Conwell kept pushing the envelope of *what is* until his ideas blossomed into *what could be?* I'm sure there was someone on his church board of directors who said, "You can't do that, Russell. Let me explain some realities to you." And I'm sure Conwell listened to all the facts.

But Conwell believed in his dreams so much that the facts didn't count! If you look at the facts, 57 cents doesn't go very far, does it? That's just a fact. But a dream—that's a different matter! Because of a dream, 57 cents wasn't the sad end of a little girl's life. Because of a dream, 57 cents was the beginning of a major building campaign!

## Five Kinds of Dreamers

As I see it, there are five kinds of people in this world. I'm sure you'll recognize yourself in one or more of these categories. Let's take a brief look at each one:

1) **Dream Makers:** Dream Makers are the men and women who dream and then do whatever it takes to make their dreams come true. These are the people I focus on in this book.

2) **Dream Bakers:** These are dreamers who are always cooking up new dreams. As soon as they accomplish one dream, they pop some more dreams into the oven.

3) **Dream Fakers:** These are people who say they have dreams, but they never do anything to make them come true. Dream Fakers don't "fake it 'til they make it." They just fake it....

4) **Dream Undertakers:** These are people who bury their dreams, rationalizing that if you don't dream, you can't be disappointed if your dream doesn't come true.

5) **Dream Takers:** These are toxic people who think they can lift themselves up by tearing other people down. Beware the Dream Takers, because they'll give you every reason in the world your dreams won't come true!

Now, as you re-read these categories, ask yourself, "Which category of dreamer best describes me?" It'd be wonderful if most people identified themselves in the first two categories—Dream Maker or Dream Baker. But it's my observation that most people fall into the last three categories—Dream Fakers, Undertakers, and Takers. Here's how I think the categories rank among the general population:

Dream Makers & Bakers—20%

Dream Takers, Fakers & Undertakers—80%

## Attention All 80%-ers—This Book Is for YOU!

Truth be told, I wrote this book mainly for two kinds of people: *Dream Fakers,* people who have dreams but can't seem to make them come true; and *Dream Undertakers,* people who have buried their dreams because they're afraid of failure. If you learn and apply the strategies in this book, you, too, can live your dreams!

If you're a Dream Faker, that's good, because you already know how to dream. What this book will do for you is to help you actualize those dreams.

As for you Dream Undertakers, I understand your reluctance to dream. Hey, I've been there. When I lacked confidence in myself, I buried a bunch of my dreams. But each time I achieved something that was a bit of a reach, I gained confidence in my ability to become a Dream Maker, whether it was winning a tennis match against an opponent I didn't think I could beat or remodeling a house, even though I didn't know the difference between a table saw and a tablespoon when I started.

> But a man who doesn't dream is like a man who doesn't sweat. He stores up a lot of poison.
>
> –Truman Capote, *The Grass Harp* (1951)

That's not to say the strategies in this book can't help Dream Makers and Dream Bakers—even the best can always get better, and the strategies in this book can help the Makers and Bakers lift themselves up to a whole new level.

## Beware the Dream Takers!

As for the Dream Takers, well, I've found out the hard way that it's better to avoid toxic people than to get contaminated trying to clean them up! I'm not saying *every* Dream Taker can't be saved, but the danger in investing your time trying to convert a Dream Taker into a Dream Maker is that *you may be the one who gets converted to their side!*

I hate to say it, but Dream Takers are like vampires—they get nourishment from draining the dreams from other people. Sorry to tell you this, but it's been my experience that it's best to avoid Dream Vampires, because they have a lot better chance of bringing you down than you have of building them up. Sad truth is, fish gotta swim. That's what fish do. And Dream Takers gotta drain other people's dreams.

That's what they do. You may be immune to their bite, but why take the chance? My advice for handling Dream Takers is this: Be polite. Be positive. Beware. And then *be gone!*

## Instead of Lowering Expectations, Increase Strategies!

A recent *USA Today* article pointed out the gap between having dreams and making them come true. According to a Junior Achievement survey of middle- and high-school students, three out of four boys and one of three girls believe they'll be millionaires by their 40th birthday. The survey went on to reveal that the two fastest growing career choices for students are the Internet and "entertainer," which doubled in popularity in two years.

Wow! Talk about big dreams. More than half the students between 12 and 18 dream of earning millions of dollars in glamorous careers. You can't say these kids are Dream Undertakers, can you? They have big dreams, big time!

But the *USA Today* article didn't congratulate the kids for having big dreams. Instead, the article *criticized the students for having unrealistic expectations* and quoted a job counselor as saying, "Those are among 'some disturbing findings in the poll about student expectations.'"

What I find disturbing isn't the kids' expectations—it's the counselor's negative attitude! The solution to helping kids make their dreams come true isn't to teach them to lower their expectations. *The solution to helping kids make their dreams come true is to teach them the strategies they'll need to become Dream Makers in a dream-taking world!*

Can you imagine this counselor advising Bill Gates or Michael Dell to lower their expectations because there's no way they can become millionaires by age 40? Or how about advising Barbra Streisand or Garth Brooks to lower their expectations because being an entertainer is an unrealistic dream. Hey, who's this counselor who makes, maybe, $40,000 a year (if he's lucky) to advise kids to lower their expectations?

Truth is, we don't need more Dream Takers like this counselor encouraging our children to lower their expectations. What we need is more Dream Makers teaching our children the proven strategies they'll need to practice to make their dreams come true!

All I know is this—if Russell H. Conwell had listened to this counselor, Temple University wouldn't even exist. If Walt Disney had listened to this counselor, the counselor would be taking his kids to Coney Island for their summer vacation instead of Walt Disney World, because there wouldn't *be* a Walt Disney World!

If you're serious about learning how to push the envelope of your expectations and live your dreams, who would you rather have as a mentor? A Dream Making minister with 57 cents in his pocket? Or a dream-taking counselor with a firm grip on reality?

I know which person I'd want on my dream team!

What about you?...

STRATEGY **2**

# Rope-a-Dope and You'll Always Have Hope

*It's scary to change your life. But a great career should fit into your life, not the other way around. At least give your dreams a chance.*

-Shana Spooner,
career coach

Do you remember the origins of "rope-a-dope"?

The term goes back to the days following Muhammad Ali's victory over George Foreman in the 1974 heavyweight championship fight held in Kinshasa, Zaire (now the Republic of the Congo), that Ali dubbed, "The Rumble in the Jungle."

The 32-year-old Ali was past his prime, although he occasionally showed traces of his nimble footwork and lightning-fast jab. Foreman was at his peak, a 25-year-old power-puncher who was undefeated in 40 professional fights, most won by early-round knockouts. It was the classic matchup between the cagey boxer, Ali-the-brains and the brutal slugger, Foreman-the-brawn.

In the second round, Ali leaned his back against the ropes and invited Foreman to hit him. Foreman obliged, throwing round-house punches that Ali deflected with his gloves and forearms. The announcers and the crowd were screaming. If a boxer was on the ropes, it meant he was in trouble, but Ali was entreating Foreman to slug him while he was on the ropes. What was Ali thinking, anyway?

*"Get off the ropes!"* the pro-Ali crowd screamed. *"Get off the ropes!"*

Near the end of the eighth round, it was obvious that Foreman was exhausted from throwing dozens of bombs. Suddenly, Ali came off the ropes with a flurry of punches, catching Foreman square on the jaw with a right hand. Foreman crumpled to the canvas and lay flat on his back with his arms and legs spread like a child resting after making a snow angel. The referee counted out the "invincible" George Foreman as the jubilant crowd chanted, "Ali! Ali! Ali! Ali!"

## Change a Losing Strategy

When interviewed after the fight, Ali said he intentionally leaned against the ropes and referred to his new-found strategy as the "rope-a-dope." Ali contended that he had planned the rope-a-dope strategy months prior to the fight, though many boxing experts disagreed, theorizing that Ali had adopted the strategy in the heat of battle.

I'm more concerned with *why* Ali adopted his rope-a-dope strategy than when, for Ali's unorthodox strategy teaches us this valuable lesson: Dream Makers abandon losing strategies and try new ones, even if they're unconventional.

That's what *Strategy #2: Rope a Dope and You'll Always Have Hope* is all about—successful people will drop an old, losing strategy in favor of a new, winning strategy, even if the new strategy is untested and unorthodox.

Now, I realize that some people don't care for Ali's politics or personality. Please understand that I'm not trying to hold him up as a role model. I'm just trying to use the story behind the very famous rope-a-dope phrase to paint a vivid word picture of a very serious strategy—*Rope-a-dope and you'll always have hope.* Dream Makers understand, in other words, that if Strategy A isn't working, then it's time to go to Strategy B.

The world-famous author Mark Twain, for example, developed a painful case of carpal tunnel syndrome in his right hand and couldn't write for weeks on end. Quitting writing was not an option for Twain, for he was a habitual writer, working five hours every morning, seven days a week, for decades. So Twain switched to Strategy B—*he taught himself to write with his left hand!* A few years later, he changed strategies again, switching from hand-writing his books to typing them on a manual typewriter. Twain was proud of his adaptability, and he openly bragged that he was the first writer to submit a typed manuscript to a publisher.

## Your Results Are Only As Good As Your Strategies

This is a good time to take a moment to talk about strategies and why they're so important. The word *strategy* comes from a Greek word for generalship; that is, the battle plan for moving combat forces and equipment into the most advantageous position before the actual battle begins.

Hannibal's strategy of launching a surprise attack against the Romans by crossing the Alps with 57 elephants is a classic example of creative, effective generalship. Despite being outmanned, Hannibal won the battle because of his superior strategy.

The military metaphor is a good one to explain the importance of strategies, because, in effect, each of us is the commanding general of our own lives, wouldn't you agree? Each of us dreams of the territory we want to lay claim to (our home and lifestyle), and then we formulate strategies to get what we want. What strategies people choose determines whether they get what they dream of… or whether they fall far short.

To better understand the importance of strategies, let's look at some *good dreams* that people have and then look at the typical *bad strategies* they use to make those dreams come true.

People dream of reducing stress in their lives. So what strategy do most people use to relax in the evening? They sit in front of the TV for four hours a night snacking on junk food. *Good dream, bad strategy.*

> I like the dreams of the future better than the history of the past.
>
> –Thomas Jefferson

People dream of retiring early with plenty of money to travel and do what they want. So what strategy do millions of people use to become financially free? They buy several hundred dollars of lottery tickets each month. *Good dream, bad strategy.*

People dream of calling their own shots and making their own decisions in life. So what strategy do most people use to become free? They trade their time and talents for a nine-to-five job that helps the company's owners build their dream of freedom. *Good dream, bad strategy.*

People dream of enjoying a comfortable lifestyle. So what strategy do most consumers use? They run up an average of $8,000 in credit card bills at 18% interest to buy stuff today that loses 90% of its value tomorrow. *Good dream, bad strategy.*

*Now, what's really sad about these strategies is that they're so common!* Let's face it, most Americans are out of shape... out of money... out of hope... and in debt up to their eyeballs! *What's wrong with this picture?*

## Change Your Strategies, Change Your Life

Why do so many people have good dreams but bad strategies to make them come true? Because they learn their strategies from family and friends who are making the same strategic mistakes! In other words, they're learning their "success" strategies from Dream Takers and Dream Undertakers, not Dream Makers. No wonder so many people are having a hard time making their dreams come true!

Successful professionals and independent business owners, on the other hand, use proven, surefire strategies for making their dreams come true. It's a simple matter of cause and effect—good strategies get good results. Bad strategies get bad results. It stands to reason that if you replace bad strategies with good ones, you'll get the same results that Dream Makers get. It's as simple as that!

That's why Dream Makers use the rope-a-dope strategy—when they realize their battle to win their dreams isn't going according to plan, they change strategies. The people who don't change strategies, on the other hand, end up being "the dope," exhausted and defeated, like George Foreman was back in 1974.

## Life Plays Tricks on Us

From time to time, we all employ strategies that don't work. Even the best-laid strategies can end up bombing. Sometimes it's not the fault of the strategies. Sometimes life just doesn't cooperate with our plans. It's like the old joke: "Do you know how to make God laugh? Tell Him your plans!"

Remember—we live in a dream-taking world. So we have to be prepared to change strategies when things aren't going our way. As the writer Franz Kafka once quipped, "In a battle between you and the world, I'll bet on the world." In other words, since life isn't going to adjust to us, we have to adjust to life. That's why we have to remain flexible and rope-a-dope if we want to have hope.

Ironically, sometimes what we think are setbacks in life turn out to blessings in disguise. (Let's face it, life may be unpredictable, but it's never dull!) All too often, life is like the old "that's good, no, that's bad" joke. The joke opens with a young woman telling a friend about her new husband:

"I just got married," the young woman says.

"*That's good,*" replies her friend.

"Yeah, but he's 40 years older than me."

*"That's bad."*

"But he's a billionaire."

*"That's good."*

"Problem is, he won't give me any money to spend."

*"That's bad."*

"But he bought me a fabulous mansion to live in."

*"That's good."*

"Not really. The mansion burned down last week."

*"That's bad."*

"No, *that's good.* He was in it!"

The joke reminds us that sometimes life plays tricks on us. What we think is good for us, turns out bad, and what we think is bad, turns out to be good. It's like the old saw, "Be careful what you wish for because you might get it!"

This is why it's so crucial that you understand and practice the rope-a-dope strategy—all too often, things don't go according to plan. And when that happens, you have to be prepared to move in a different direction.

## A Broken Promise Leads to a Big Dream

There are millions of stories about Dream Makers who have had to rope-a-dope and change strategies in mid-stream in order to make their dreams come true. One of my favorite stories is about Truett Cathy, the legendary founder of the Chick-fil-A franchises.

Truett got his start in business after his discharge from the service at the end of WWII. Truett and his brother, Ben, wanted to go into business together, but they couldn't decide what type. Then one day the manager of a restaurant called The Dutch Kitchen introduced Truett and Ben to the owner, who had plans to expand into a chain of restaurants around the Atlanta area.

The owner recognized the young men's ambition and hired them for a training period, promising each a restaurant to manage upon completion of their "internship." The Cathy brothers worked 12 hours a day, seven days a week, for seven weeks at The Dutch Kitchen. But at the end of the trial period, the owner refused to live up to her part of the bargain, suggesting instead that the brothers manage one restaurant together. Fortunately, their dream was much bigger than her offer, so they did what Dream Makers do—they rope-a-doped and changed strategies. *They decided to open their own restaurant!*

Changing their strategy from managing someone else's restaurant to owning their own was a breakthrough decision for the Cathy brothers, and it eventually led to the opening of the first Chick-fil-A restaurant in 1967. Today Chick-fil-A has over 1,000 restaurants—and the franchise is still growing like gangbusters!

## Add a Wrinkle to a Favorite Pair of Pants

As you will learn in Strategy #4, Dream Makers don't have to re-invent the wheel—all they have to do is follow on the train tracks laid down by the pioneers. However, sometimes we need to freshen up tried-and-true strategies with a creative wrinkle or two. Here's a story of a saleswoman who used a clever strategy to win a very big account.

> The hardest thing is just to start. Too many people have a wonderful dream and just talk about it rather than do something about it.
>
> –Debbie Fields, founder, Mrs. Field's Cookies

Shannon Bradley, a sales executive with Sun Microsoft, had been trying for several months to set an appointment with the Vice President of a data storage company. She called him every day. She sat in his office. She even went to see his boss. But she could never get the VP to meet with her. Dream Makers understand that persistence is a key strategy for success, but persistence was getting Bradley nowhere. So she rope-a-doped and tried a slightly different strategy. Instead of phoning or sending an invitation to lunch, Bradley sent the

VP a shoe with a note in it that said, "Now that I have my foot in the door, will you have lunch with me?" Five minutes later the VP called her back on her cell phone and set up a meeting. She closed the deal a few days later.

"We had the right technology at the right time," Bradley said. "But if you don't get to the guy with the money, it doesn't matter. You've got to get in the door."

Dream Fakers and Undertakers give up in the face of daily rejection. But Bradley was a Dream Maker, and she kept going until she found a strategy that worked.

## Dream Makers See the Handwriting on the Wall

Persistence is crucial to making your dream come true, but Dream Makers understand that sometimes you have to make a 180-degree turn if you're serious about making your dreams come true.

We all know unfulfilled doctors, lawyers, and accountants, for example, who quit their professions in order to make their dreams come true. Several recent surveys indicate that 40% of attorneys would change careers if they were presented with a good opportunity. I know attorneys who are now playing in rock bands, and members of rock bands who are now attorneys. The key to becoming a Dream Maker is to have the wisdom to admit it when a strategy isn't working, and then have the courage to change to a strategy that does work for you.

Lawrence Small, the president of Fannie Mae, the giant federally backed mortgage lender, is a great example of someone who made a 180-degree flip-flop in his Dream Making strategy. As a freshman in college, Small overheard a recording of flamenco guitar music in his dorm room. It was love at first hearing, and the guitar-playing freshman decided that his dream was to become "the world's greatest flamenco guitarist." He studied flamenco guitar for two years, including a year in Spain living with gypsies. Then he stepped back and examined his dream:

"The top 10 flamenco guitarists were all ethnic gypsies who'd hit the stage before they were 12. All were under five-foot-seven, had black hair, and at least one gold tooth. Two were literate and three were making a living. What were the chances for a six-foot-three-inch blond from New York?" he recalls.

Small returned to school and eventually carved out a brilliant career in finance. But because he was willing to rope-a-dope to a completely different career strategy, he still gets to indulge his passion for flamenco. To this day he practices half an hour every morning on his four guitars, and occasionally he hauls his guitar onto the corporate jet and plays lightning-fast flamenco riffs at 20,000 feet.

## Know the Difference Between the Vehicle and the Destination

There are lots of people who are like Lawrence Small when he was a star-struck college freshman—they have a big dream, and they go after it with gusto. But all too often, people confuse the vehicle with the destination. For example, many people who dream of becoming doctors or lawyers become disillusioned with their professions, but they refuse to change careers for fear they're abandoning their dream.

But what they fail to realize is that more often than not, their *real dream* was to earn a big income while helping people. Becoming a doctor or lawyer was just the vehicle to living their dream. Once they realize their profession was just a means to an end, not an end in itself, they're free to pursue other careers that can deliver their dream.

There are zillions of examples of famous Dream Makers who boldly switched strategies in order to make their dreams come true. Here are a few of the notables:

- **Alfred Nobel,** the inventor of dynamite, went from being known as "the merchant of death" to "the man of peace" when he switched his Dream Making strategies from earning fabulous amounts of money to giving all of it away via the Nobel Prizes, awarded each year to "people who have rendered the greatest service to mankind."

- **Samuel Morse** was a talented artist whose mission was to improve the taste of Americans. Unfortunately, the public didn't appreciate Morse's talents, so he switched his Dream Making strategy from art to invention. His invention of the Morse code connected every city in America from New York to San Francisco and ushered in the Information Age.
- **James Michener** was a 40-year-old, lifetime government employee bored with his job when he decided to pursue his dream of writing. On weekends and evenings, he wrote a novel about his experiences during the war, calling it *Tales of the South Pacific.* The book was an instant bestseller, and by the time he died at age 90, he had authored 43 books. During his lifetime, he donated $100 million to colleges and writing programs.

What about you—have you ever considered making a major switch in your Dream Making strategies? Perhaps you're like one of the people above—unproductive or unfulfilled in your current career. If your current career isn't the right vehicle to deliver your dreams, *instead of giving up on your dreams, maybe you need to change vehicles!*

If Michener had given up on his dream, millions of people would have been deprived of seeing Rodgers and Hammerstein's classic musical *South Pacific,* based on Michener's first book... or reading any of his dozens of bestselling novels. Michener's decision to change careers in mid-life is proof that it's better to switch Dream Making strategies than to abandon your dreams.

After all, you can always find another winning strategy.

But you only get one chance to live your dreams!

STRATEGY 3

# Make Sure You're Milking the Right Cow

*It's never too late to be who you might have been.*

–Mary Ann Evans, a.k.a. George Eliot,
British author

"We *will bury you!*" the speaker shouted, pounding the podium with his fist.

The speaker was Nikita Khrushchev, premier of the Soviet Union. The year was 1956. America and the Soviet Union—two super powers with vastly different views of the world—were frozen in a Cold War of disagreement and distrust.

Khrushchev's 21-year-old son, Sergei, sat quietly in the audience as his father denounced America, shouting again and again that one day soon, Soviet communism would triumph over American capitalism.

Three years later, Khrushchev and his son began a 13-day trip across the United States. The trip opened Sergei's eyes. There were no soldiers in the streets. People were warm and friendly. And there were rows upon rows of pretty, painted houses with wide green lawns.

The Soviet premier and his son returned to the Soviet Union, where Sergei resided for the next 25 years. But Sergei's brief visit profoundly changed his view of America. Secretly, he dreamed of returning to the land of pretty, painted houses for a longer stay. A much longer stay....

## Why I Love America!

In 1986, 30 years after his first visit to the United States, Sergei Khrushchev was offered a fellowship to teach at Brown University in Providence, Rhode Island. He jumped at the opportunity to return to America. He soon settled into middle class life, teaching and touring the States on speaking engagements. The more Sergei saw of the States and the longer he stayed, the more he liked it.

> If you have a dream and don't follow it you'll regret it for a long, long time.
>
> –Norm Brodsky, columnist, *Inc.* magazine

In fact, Sergei grew to love the United States. In July of 1999, Sergei Khrushchev, the only son of a former premier of the Soviet Union, did the unthinkable. *He was sworn in as a citizen of the United States of America!*

"The great thing about this country is that people aren't trying to suppress their neighbors," Sergei said at a press conference following the citizenship ceremony he attended with his wife.

Today Sergei lives in Cranston, Rhode Island, where he teaches and writes. He lives in a modest three-bedroom wood house painted white. The tidy front lawn is the envy of the neighborhood.

"I like to take care of my home," Sergei enthuses. "It's the same with this country. I could have just stayed here with a green card, but my wife and I decided to be responsible—to live here, to vote, not just to consume. People ask me why I became a citizen. It's not political. It's personal. I feel very proud to be in this country."

## Dreams and Beliefs Must Go Hand in Hand

Now, I want you to ponder the full significance of Sergei Khrushchev becoming an American citizen. Think about it—*the son of the former leader of the most powerful communist government in the world is now living the American Dream!* How ironic is that?!!! Truth is certainly stranger than fiction, isn't it?

What compelled Sergei Khrushchev, a 64-year-old man who was taught all of his life to hate America, to switch sides and declare his allegiance to a sworn enemy? The answer is that Sergei Khrushchev came to realize that the only thing standing between him and his dreams was an old Soviet mindset that didn't work for him anymore. Once he opened his mind, a flood of new hopes and dreams rushed in, sweeping away the clutter of a deeply flawed doctrine called communism.

What can we learn from the story of Sergei Khrushchev? The biggest lesson we learn is that our dreams have to be in concert with our belief system. Sergei's dream was to teach and write without censorship, but that wasn't possible under the Soviet system, even today.

"I still had to deal with bureaucrats in the 'new' Soviet Union," Sergei bristles. "I still had to say not what I was thinking but what I was *supposed* to think. In this country, there was no censorship. I could write what I wanted and publish every word!"

So, in order for Sergei to become a Dream Maker, he had to change his thinking. His old thinking—"don't rock the communist party boat"—allowed no room for him to realize his dream of writing freely and uncensored. So he was faced with a choice. Give up his dreams. Or give up his old way of thinking. Sergei wisely chose to keep his dreams!

Sergei was practicing *Strategy #3* for realizing your dreams: *Make Sure You're Milking the Right Cow*. You see, the sick and dying Soviet cow just wasn't designed to deliver the milk that Sergei needed to nurture his dreams. So he switched cows. As long as he stayed in the Soviet

Union—either physically or mentally—he would always remain a Dream Undertaker because his dreams were incompatible with the Soviet system. But once he adopted the mindset of his new country, the Dream Maker in him was set free!

## Ask Yourself, "Is It Working?"

What about you?—are you milking the right cow? Or are you clinging to a mindset that is at odds with your dreams? If your mindset is to have a secure job, but your dream is to sail around the world before you're 50, you're faced with a dilemma because you can't do both! As my friend Burke would say, "You can't steal second with your foot on first."

Phil McGraw, better known as "Dr. Phil" on Oprah Winfrey's talk show, has a simple strategy for people to open their minds and get rid of outdated, counterproductive thinking:

"Instead of asking yourself whether the way you are living, behaving, and thinking *is right,* ask yourself whether the way you are living, behaving, and thinking *is working or not working.* I suggest that if what you are choosing is not working, that by itself tells you that those things are worthy of change. Whatever your situation, there is a strategy that will make you a winner."

Dr. Phil's advice certainly gets to the heart of the matter, doesn't it? If your dream is to own a house on the beach but your "safe and secure" job only pays you $35,000 a year, you've got a problem, don't you? I mean, something's got to give! Sadly, for most people, what gives is their dream.

It never ceases to amaze me how many people bury their dreams for what they think is a safe, secure job. Here's proof. The Gallup Poll recently finished interviewing 110,000 government employees regarding their job satisfaction. The majority of workers are what Gallup calls *"ROAD Warriors"*—**R**etired **O**n **A**ctive **D**uty. Gallup Vice President Donald Beck says the most frequent comment from workers was something like this:

*"I really hate my job, but I only have 20 more years before retirement."*

Wow!—is that an eye opener, or what? Tens of thousands of people are putting their dreams on dry ice for 20 years in exchange for a secure job they hate! How sad is that? These people are not only milking the wrong cow, they hate the cow they're milking but are volunteering to pull up a stool at eight o'clock every morning anyway. What a waste of time and talent! I've got to believe that most of those people have a Dream Maker inside of them struggling to get out.

Truth is, Dream Makers don't give up their dream—they just keep searching until they find a bigger, healthier cow to milk. Take a look at the cows some famous Dream Makers were milking before they found their dream cow:

> **James Earl Jones,** Academy Award winning actor, waxed floors for a living.
>
> **Rodney Dangerfield,** the "I-don't-get-no-respect" comedian, sold aluminum siding until he was 40 years old.
>
> **Jerry Seinfeld,** TV star and comedian, sold light bulbs on the phone.
>
> **Harry Truman,** 33rd president of the United States, failed as a farmer and store owner before entering politics full time.
>
> **Ralph Lauren,** founder of Polo clothing, sold ties in a men's store in Manhattan.
>
> **Roberta Flack,** singer and entertainer, taught grade school.
>
> **Berry Gordy,** founder of Motown Records, worked the night shift at an automobile plant in Detroit.
>
> **Bob Newhart,** long-time comedian and TV star, worked as a copywriter for an advertising agency in Chicago.

What all of these people had in common was a big dream and the courage and common sense to abandon the cows that couldn't deliver their dreams. I bet Bob Newhart struggled with his decision to give up a paycheck to chase his dream. Same with Rodney Dangerfield and Roberta Flack. But what do you think would have happened to these people if they'd played it safe and kept their jobs instead of chasing their "unrealistic" dream? Do you think they'd be happy and fulfilled? We both know the answer to that....

## Beware the Whirling Disease!

When people choose to cling to a "secure," dead-end job instead of chasing their dreams, it reminds me of something called the "whirling disease," which is threatening to wipe out the rainbow trout population in Montana and Colorado. Experts think the disease blossomed in the state fish hatcheries, where the safe, controlled environment enabled the contaminated "domesticated" fish to grow until they were released into the streams and rivers, thereby spreading the disease to the wild rainbow population.

Here's how the devastating disease gets its name: Protozoa enter the trout and settle in the fish's cartilage. The protozoa grow by feeding on the cartilage near the fish's tail, deforming the weakened tail into a permanent curve. When the fish try to swim forward, the curved tail causes them to spin frantically in small circles until they die. Thus, the name the whirling disease.

Although the whirling disease is limited to rainbow trout, many cautious humans exhibit the same symptoms—they keep spinning in circles, never advancing forward, no matter how hard they try! You see, like the domesticated rainbow trout, many Dream Fakers and Undertakers seek out safe, secure work environments, where the "protozoa" of doubt and fear enter their system and grow. Instead of challenging themselves to negotiate the rapids of reality, people with the whirling disease hang back in a controlled environment, choosing to live and work in what they think is a safe, secure pool of life. They tell themselves they're trying to swim toward their dreams, but in reality, they're destined to swim in circles until they die.

The reason so many people suffer from the whirling disease is they want to have it both ways—they want to stay in the safe confines of the hatchery, but they also want to dart and play in the river with the Dream Making fish. News flash—you can't have it both ways!

James Earl Jones, for example, realized he couldn't remain a janitor and pursue his dream of acting at the same time. He had a choice: He could play it safe and fall victim to the whirling disease. Or he could immunize himself against the whirling disease by becoming a Dream Maker. Jones chose to follow his impossible dream instead of following a floor polishing machine for the rest of his life. The result? A distinguished 30-year career on stage and in film and numerous awards, including an Academy Award nomination.

## Whirling Disease Affects Professionals, too!

The reason I'm so familiar with the whirling disease is because I used to be caught in its insidious grip! For the last 10 years of my 16-year teaching career, I had a serious case of the whirling disease. I wasn't happy teaching. I didn't feel I was taking full advantage of my God-given talents. I felt confined. I was bored, all too often going through the motions for a monthly paycheck. And, I must admit, I had fallen under the spell of the three biggest benefits of teaching—June, July, and August! I used to tell myself that summers off justified the low pay I got from the school board and the low respect I got from the students. But that was just a rationalization for not having the courage to follow my dream. Truth is, I had a bad case of the whirling disease, and I was spinning in small circles, like dishwater going down a drain.

> Success is the intersection where dreams and hard work meet.
>
> –Lynn Goldblatt

In all fairness, teachers aren't the only ones who catch serious cases of the whirling disease. There are tons of dissatisfied, displaced attorneys, accountants, and doctors who are whirling their lives away—and none too happy about it.

## Status Addiction Is Hard to Kick!

For sure, many dissatisfied professionals stay captive to the whirling disease for the money. But in my opinion, the vast majority of dissatisfied professionals can't kick the whirling disease because they hate to let go of the status. Sad, but true! Let's face it, telling people you're a doctor or a lawyer really raises eyebrows on the cocktail circuit. People are impressed.

But the simple truth is, all the status in the world can't cover up the elephants standing in every professional's waiting room. The elephant of the medical profession is managed care. Desperate to keep down rising medical costs, big insurance companies have chopped most docs' compensation to 50% of what it was 10 years ago—and there's no end in sight! Add to that the exorbitant cost of malpractice insurance... the enormous overhead associated with maintaining a private practice... and the ridiculously long hours most professionals have to work just to keep their heads above water—well, it's little wonder that so many professionals are kicking the cows that they once thought were sacred.

The legal profession has its own elephant in the reception room—overcrowding. There are so many attorneys today that they have to battle each other like hungry dogs for every scrap of business.

The yellow pages in my local phone book, for example, list 143 pages of attorneys (compared to only 18 pages of plumbers). New York City alone has 50,000 attorneys, and in Washington, DC, one out of every 13 workers has a law degree! Now, there's NO WAY there's enough legitimate business to go around for that many attorneys. So what happens? The courts get flooded with more and more frivolous suits brought by attorneys desperate for business.

## Whirling Disease in Humans Is Curable

Look, I don't mean to come off as an attorney basher. In this day and age, attorneys are a necessity, not an option, given that business and money matters have become so complicated. All I'm saying is that there are too many attorneys (and executives and doctors and teachers and accountants) *who remain in their profession for the wrong reasons!*

I know literally dozens of attorneys. Every one of them is talented and bright. And all of them are good at what they do. But only one of 10 really loves what they do. In other words, only one in 10 is living their dream! What a waste!

Just think—all of these talented people are going through life milking the wrong cow. Worst of all, they know it, yet most refuse to go shopping for another cow. Why? I guess they figure the cow you know is better than the cow you don't know. So they commute to the barn every morning, pull up the stool, and milk their "billable hours." Meanwhile, they keep whirling around and around in circles, hoping for the day they win the big settlement that will buy them their freedom.

Folks, the good news is that the whirling disease in humans is curable. Dream Makers are proof of that. Most Dream Makers felt trapped in a downward spiral, too, but they did what they had to do to break free and make their dreams come true.

## Dream Makers Find a Way

Bestselling author John Grisham, for example, was a successful attorney. Like many attorneys, he felt he was milking the wrong cow. But, like all of us, he lived in a dream-taking world. He had a wife and two kids to support, so he couldn't just walk away from his thriving law practice.

But Grisham refused to give in to the whirling disease. He started getting up at four o'clock every morning to write his first book, *A Time to Kill,* before heading into his law office. Once the book was finished, his struggles didn't end, for Grisham faced a whole new series of challenges. The manuscript was rejected by a dozen major publishers. Finally, a small regional publisher agreed to publish the book, but they had no money to promote it, which, in the book publishing world, is the kiss of death.

Yet Grisham was undeterred. When the book came out, he bought several thousand copies, loaded them into the trunk of his car, and set out to visit every bookstore within a day's driving distance from his home. He signed copies at garden clubs. He dropped in on small reading circles and gave books away. He lectured to writing classes. For eight months, Grisham spent every weekend hawking his book to anyone who could read.

And then a miraculous thing began to happen—as word of mouth spread, bookstores started getting requests for the book. Eventually, the book became a regional bestseller... then a national bestseller... and eventually a major Hollywood movie. All because John Grisham refused to let a dream-taking world keep him from living his dream.

## Build Your Own Dream Ladder

Jim Collins, another bestselling author who wrote the business classic, *Good to Great,* has a simple yet powerful philosophy for dissatisfied people who are looking to make a career change:

"Instead of climbing a crowded ladder," Collins asks, "why not create your own ladder and put yourself at the top?" Great idea—and when you think about it, that's exactly what Dream Makers do. They build their own dream ladder and climb through a dream-taking world until they get to the top.

Each of us has a different concept for the ladder of our dreams.

John Grisham climbed his dream ladder to the top of the bestseller list.

James Earl Jones climbed his dream ladder to stardom on stage and screen.

Sergei Khrushchev climbed his dream ladder to freedom in America.

What about you—where will your dream ladder lead to? Only you know the answer to that question. But this much is for sure. You begin by climbing one rung at a time. Sometimes the climbing is slow-going. And sometimes a dream-taking world may push you back a rung or two. But when you finally get to the top of your dream ladder, it'll be worth it. *The view is spectacular!*

STRATEGY 4

# Travel on the Train Tracks

*Saddle your dreams before you ride 'em.*

–Mary Webb,
writer & humorist

C*lang! Clang! Clang!*

The sound of a steel hammer smashing into an iron spike on May 10, 1869, sprinted across the barren landscape of Promontory Point, Utah, like a startled jack rabbit.

*Clang! Clang! Clang!*

Wires connected to the spike relayed the clanging sound to thousands of telegraph offices throughout America, and the nation cheered in unison—the transcontinental railroad track connecting New York to San Francisco was finally complete!

Talk about an "impossible dream"! It took 25,000 laborers working 10-hour days seven years to lay the final 1,700 miles of track from

Omaha to Sacramento. The mostly Irish and Chinese crews had to build dozens of bridges and blast and chop their way around and through two mountain ranges—*by hand!*

Was the dream worth the effort? Consider this: It took pioneers in wagon trains *six months and cost $1,000* to travel from coast to coast. It took passengers on the transcontinental railroad *six days and $70* to make the same trip! In other words, it *cost 14 times more money...* and it took *30 times more time* for the pioneers to accomplish the same goal as the passengers. So I ask you, which would you rather be? A pioneer? Or a passenger?

## Easier to Be a Passenger Than a Pioneer

The point of this brief history lesson is that it's a lot easier being a passenger than a pioneer. Why? Because pioneers have to take huge risks to arrive at their destination. Pioneers have to learn by trial and error, wasting valuable time and money trying to figure out what works. Pioneers take wrong turns. Pioneers get lost. And pioneers are forced to make bad decisions because they lack reliable information.

Passengers, on the other hand, get to travel on the train tracks to their destinations. Passengers take advantage of a rail system that someone else paid for with their time, money, and effort. All passengers have to do is find a travel schedule and then follow the directions. As a result, passengers arrive at their destination in less time, for less money, and with less aggravation than pioneers.

Now do you see why I say it's better to be a passenger than a pioneer?

*Strategy #4: Travel on the Train Tracks,* means that you don't have to be a genius or re-invent the wheel to live your dreams. Why be a pioneer when you can get the same results in less time with less effort as a passenger? All you have to do to live your dreams is ride the rails of Dream Makers! It doesn't get any simpler than that!

## True Story of a Passenger Riding the Rails to Success

To better understand the concept of traveling on the train tracks, I'd like to tell you the story of a WWII veteran who always had a dream of becoming a writer. After the war ended, the aspiring writer took his $900 in savings and moved to New York City, where he rented a cold-water flat just off Times Square. He wrote in the evenings and spent his days pitching his material to 50 magazines in the city. All he got for his efforts were piles of rejection slips. Finally the money ran out, and the man moved to Boston, where the only job he could find was selling insurance.

The man eventually married and the couple had a daughter. The man worked long hours, but no matter how hard he worked, there were always more bills than income. Frustrated, the man started stopping by the local bar on his way home from work. Over time, one drink after work led to two drinks... then three... then six. One day the man returned home from an insurance convention to find a note on the kitchen table. His wife and daughter had fled.

The man's life continued to spiral downhill. The bank foreclosed on his home, so he packed his clothes in his old red Ford Falcon and headed west, bouncing from job to job to keep the cheap wine flowing. Eventually he ended up in a run-down section of Cleveland, cold and miserable, filthy from living on the street. One night in a steady rain he drunkenly leaned against the window of a pawn shop to steady himself. He peered in the window to see a handgun with a $29.95 price tag. The man jabbed his hand into his pocket and pulled out three crumpled $10 bills.

He thought how easy it would be to end his misery with one gunshot. But a voice inside told him there *must* be a better way. So, he turned and walked down the rain-slick street to the nearest warm, dry place. It was a public library. He spent the evening reading in the quiet confines of the library. He was so comforted by the books and words that he returned night after night, searching for answers from the world's greatest thinkers: Aristotle, Plato, Emerson, Franklin, and scores of other original thinkers. Gradually, his drinking tapered down to an occasional beer.

Then one morning, in the main library in Concord, New Hampshire, the man discovered *Success Through a Positive Mental Attitude* by W. Clement Stone and Napoleon Hill. The message hit him like a thunderbolt: *You can accomplish anything you wish that is not contradictory to the laws of God or man, providing you are willing to pay a price.*

> You'll always pay full retail for success, but never, never discount your dreams.
>
> –Dr. Bill Quain, author and speaker

"Pay a price for your dreams," he thought as he turned the pages. "That's the difference between this book and the others."

Inspired by the book, the man traveled to Boston and applied for a salesman's job in W. Clement Stone's insurance company. The man was 35 years old and flat broke. But he had a dream and he was willing to pay a price to accomplish that dream. He quickly became their top salesman. The man eventually became the editor of the company's in-house motivational magazine, and an article he wrote was read by a publisher, who sent a letter telling the man he had talent and encouraging him to submit a manuscript for publication. Eighteen months later, the man's dream became reality—Frederick Fell Publishing bought the man's book!

## Dreams Do Come True!

You may recognize the name of the book, *The Greatest Salesman in the World.* Within four months of its publication, its sales topped 350,000 copies in hardcover and has become the bestselling book of all time in the field of sales. Although published almost 30 years ago, *the book still sells 100,000 copies a month!*

You may also recognize the name of the author—Og Mandino. Mandino went on to write 18 books with sales totaling 40 million copies (and still counting) in dozens of languages.

Now, what does this remarkable story have to do with traveling on the train tracks? Think about it—at his lowest point, Mandino was broke, drunk, and suicidal. He was anything but a pioneer! But he had the good fortune to turn to books instead of a loaded gun to solve his problems. And in the books he discovered the wisdom of some of the greatest intellectual pioneers in history. By reading the masters, he didn't have to blaze an intellectual trail. All he had to do was follow the train tracks that others had laid down for him. As a result, he was able to right himself, correct his course, and travel on the tracks until he reached his dream.

## Stop Growing, and You Stop Living

Og Mandino's life is a lesson in the power of personal growth. Mandino had hit rock bottom, but instead of giving in to despair, he sought out the knowledge and wisdom that would empower him to reinvent his life.

Just as we have to feed our bodies nutritious food in order to remain healthy and vibrant, so must we feed our minds and souls nutritious information and knowledge in order to grow personally and professionally.

It's like the story about the motivational speaker who was on a return flight from a seminar. When the speaker told the man next to him what he did for a living, the man wrinkled his brow and said, "Ah-h-h, that motivational stuff is for the birds. It doesn't last. You get yourself all pumped up for a while and then it wears off."

"*Well, a bath doesn't last either,*" the motivational speaker replied. "*But it's still a good idea to take at least one a day.*"

If you think about it, lots of stuff in our personal lives need constant replenishing. Food doesn't last. Exercise doesn't last. And productive strategies don't last, either, unless we feed and exercise them. That's what motivational and training materials do—they feed the mind so that we can live and work to our fullest potential. It's called personal growth, folks.

## Tough Love Better Than a Tender Heart

It's my observation that most people think of personal growth programs and materials in the same way as the skeptic on the airplane—that self-help principles just pump people up for a few days but don't have any lasting benefit.

*Nothing could be further from the truth!* To the contrary, personal growth is the only thing that *does last* because proven strategies and positive values are transferable from one situation to the next. Here's proof of the need for ongoing personal growth programs:

> The years forever fashion new dreams when old ones go. God pity a one-dream man.
>
> –Robert Goddard, rocket scientist

For 14 years, Metropolitan Ministries has offered free meals and shelter to homeless people in my hometown of Tampa, Florida. Good intentions. But bad results! Why? Because most of the "clients" were using the facility for a *permanent hand out,* instead of a *temporary hand up.* Yes, some of their clients were down on their luck and needed temporary assistance. But the majority were suffering from the whirling disease—they were just going around and around in a circle of alcoholism or drug addiction. Unfortunately, most of their clients had become addicted to their handouts, just as much as they were addicted to alcohol and drugs.

The leadership of Metropolitan Ministries decided their assistance program needed an overhaul. As Karlene Kos, vice president of program delivery, says, "*Sometimes you can, in the name of love, do too much for people and it allows them to stay miserable. We're moving to serve people who want to change their lives.*"

In September, 2000, Metropolitan Ministries introduced "Uplift U," a 6- to 18-month program of classes and counseling designed to help the homeless break the cycle of dependence and become self-sufficient by developing personal skills, people skills, coping skills, and job skills. In effect, Metropolitan Ministries changed their philosophy from a tender-hearted approach that *promoted pity*... to a tough-love approach that promoted *personal growth*. In a nutshell, they switched from "giving a man a fish" to "teaching a man to fish."

Today, down-and-out people who need a hand up because of bad choices or bad luck can learn the strategies and skills necessary to regain control of their lives. But as for the hopeless losers who've been getting a handout for years without any strings attached—sorry, but there's no more free lunch at Metropolitan Ministries for Freddie the Freeloaders!

## What About Developing Your Own Uplift U Program?

What about your own life? Are you stuck in a rut littered with ineffective strategies, outmoded skills, and outdated thinking? Or are you enrolled in your own Uplift U personal growth program?

It's my observation that Dream Makers are permanently enrolled in a self-directed Uplift U. They're always looking to improve their productivity. Improve their marriage. Improve their fitness. Improve their relationships. Improve their communication skills. Improve their knowledge. Improve their attitude.

There are as many courses of study in your Uplift U as there are Dream Makers in this world, but as I see it, there are three main ways to travel on the Uplift U train tracks:

1) Find a mentor

2) Attend live seminars, events, and classes

3) Get information from books, tapes, CD ROMs, and the Internet

The purpose of any personal Uplift U program is to acquire the knowledge and the skills and to adopt the strategies that will empower you to use your full potential. That's all Og Mandino did, and it turned his life around 180 degrees.

Think about it—Mandino had the same talents and abilities before he hit rock bottom that he had afterwards. He sold insurance before he became an alcoholic. He wrote stories before he became an alcoholic. His talents didn't change, did they? What changed? *His strategies!*

You see, Og failed as a writer and failed as an insurance agent NOT because he lacked talent, but because he was practicing the wrong strategies! Once he traveled the train tracks and learned the strategies of Dream Makers, he began to apply those strategies to his life. What happened? The second time he tried his hand at selling insurance using proven success strategies, he zoomed to the top of the sales organization! And once he started using more successful strategies as a writer, his books started selling like hotcakes!

In the first scenario, the same person fails miserably. In the second scenario a few years later, the same person succeeds beyond his wildest dreams! What's the common denominator?—*better strategies!* And better strategies get better results, it's as simple as that!

That's why I encourage you to travel on the train tracks laid down by Dream Makers. Do what the Og Mandinos of the world do to turn their lives around—seek out mentors who have done what you dream of doing. Read the books that give you wisdom and insights. Attend classes and seminars that teach you the strategies and skills you'll need to succeed. And listen to the audio tapes and watch the videos that take you to the next level.

Hey, I look at it this way—if traveling on the train tracks can turn the life of a hopeless alcoholic with $30 in his pockets into an international bestselling author, just think of what it can do for you!

*All aboard!*

STRATEGY 5

# Shop for Shoes, Not Excuses

*People are always blaming circumstances for what they are. I don't believe in circumstances. The people who get along in this world are the people who, if they don't like their circumstances, go out and create their own.*

—George Bernard Shaw,
author and social critic

Born with a degenerative eye disease, Erik Weihenmayer could only see shapes and shadows by the time he was seven. But that didn't prevent the irrepressible youngster from playing his favorite sport, basketball. What Erik lacked in eyesight, he made up for in enthusiasm. He made himself into a defensive specialist, waiving his arms wildly as he guarded opponents.

One game Erik intercepted a pass and dribbled the length of the floor for an easy lay-up. As the crowd cheered him on, Erik shot the ball toward what he thought was the basket. Turned out to be the scoreboard, and the crowd hushed as the ball bounced out of bounds.

Humiliated, Erik slunk to the bench.

The next day, Erik and his father returned to the court. Erik could see the painted sidelines, so the father and son paced the court together, counting the steps from sideline to sideline. It wasn't long before Erik could always figure out his position on the floor during a game.

Erik didn't realize it at the time, but his father was teaching him a strategy that would serve him well for the rest of his life. The strategy was this: *The solution isn't for Erik to quit. The solution is for Erik to figure out how he can participate.*

In essence, Erik's father was teaching his son the key principle behind this book, namely, that Dream Makers succeed not because they have an absence of problems but because they have an abundance of strategies that empower them to succeed.

## A Summit Ain't All About the View

No one would argue that Erik Weihenmayer will face huge challenges in life as a result of his blindness. But even though Erik is blind, he "dreams with his eyes wide open"—that is, he dreams big dreams... he assesses the challenges... and then he develops a plan that would allow him to accomplish his dreams. Because Erik practices Dream Making strategies, he has the tools and the confidence to not only do things that sighted people do, but to take on challenges that most sighted people would consider too dangerous!

Erik's biggest dream, for example, was to become a world-class mountain climber, despite the fact that he'd lost all of his eyesight in his early teens. In May of 2001, 32-year-old Erik Weihenmayer realized a dream that very few people have ever attempted, much less accomplished. *He completed a two-month climb to the top of Mount Everest, the world's highest mountain!* While the other climbers shouted with exhilaration as they looked at the view from the summit, Erik celebrated by listening.

"I could hear the beautiful sound of space around me. I heard the snapping of the Sherpa prayer flags in the wind. I touched the snow. It's a beautiful place."

For sure, Erik is a special person. It takes exceptional discipline, endurance, and will power to climb the world's highest peak. But if his father had given in to the realities of a dream-taking world and limited Erik to "safe" activities when he was growing up, there's no way he would have developed his full potential. But because Erik's father had the courage and wisdom to encourage him to push the envelope of his expectations, Erik learned to become a creative, courageous Dream Maker, instead of a timid, "realistic" Dream Undertaker.

> There are those people who will reply that freedom of man and mind is nothing but a dream. They are right. It is. It is the American Dream.
>
> –Archibald MacLeish, American poet

Despite blindness, Erik Weihenmayer has certainly accomplished dozens of his dreams. He's a college graduate. A teacher in a private school. And world-class climber who has already conquered four of the world's highest mountains on his quest to climb the "Seven Summits," the highest peaks on each continent.

"Reaching a summit ain't all about the view," Erik Weihenmayer says during his speeches to college students and corporate leaders. "A summit is a symbol that you can do what you want with your life."

## Make Excuses or Make Dreams

We can learn a lot from the Erik Weihenmayers of this world—the people who are dealt tremendous setbacks in life but who rise above them to become Dream Makers, instead of giving in to reality and becoming Dream Undertakers. So the question becomes, "What strategy empowers people like Erik Weihenmayer to overcome tremendous adversity and live their dreams?"

The answer—*Dream Makers refuse to make excuses!*

You see, we all have a choice. We can make excuses. Or we can make our dreams come true. But we can't do both. It's as simple as that. That's why *Strategy #5* for realizing your dreams is *"Shop for Shoes, Not Excuses."*

I first heard this rule from my friend Dr. Bill Quain, who, by the way, is also a big-time Dream Maker and Dream Baker despite being legally blind. For starters, he's a college professor... a sought-after speaker... an in-demand consultant... a bestselling author... a successful entrepreneur... a crackerjack fisherman... and, if that's not enough, he's also the host of a TV cooking show for visually impaired people called, *Cookin' without Lookin'* (which should tell you something about Bill's sense of humor).

I was talking to Bill about how some people will accept almost any excuse for giving up on their dreams.

"Yeah," Bill joined in. "Some people shop until they find the excuse that fits, as if they were shopping for shoes, and then they buy the excuse that's most comfortable in order to justify their giving up." Boy, is that ever the truth.

## Any Excuse Will Do

The excuses people buy into to justify their giving up on their dreams reminds me of the old joke about the guy who goes over to his neighbor's house to borrow a lawn mower.

"Can I borrow your lawn mower?" the neighbor asks politely.

"Sorry, but I can't let you borrow it. My wife's cooking Beef Stroganoff."

"What's Beef Stroganoff have to do with lending me your lawn mower?" the perplexed neighbor asks.

"Well, I don't want to loan you my lawn mower, and when you don't want to do something, any excuse will do," comes the reply.

The same goes for Dream Fakers and Dream Undertakers—if they're not actively pursuing their dreams, there's a good chance that they've shopped around until they found the excuse they need:

"I don't have the money"...

"I don't have the time"...

"I'm too busy"...

"The kids are still in school"...

"I'm too old"...

"We're having new carpeting put in"...

Yadda, yadda, yadda. If one excuse wears out, they'll shop for another. Just like shopping for shoes.

Meanwhile, the dream house they always talk about never gets built. The dream car they always wanted to drive never gets bought. The dream college they always wanted to send the kids to never gets applied to. The dream business they always longed to own never gets off the ground. You get the picture.

## My Excuses Could Have Cost Me My Dream

How about you—have you ever shopped around for an excuse until you found the one that fits? Maybe you gave up on your dream of getting back into shape with the excuse that the people at the gym aren't very friendly. Or the excuse that you'd have to eat dinner an hour later. Or the excuse that you're too tired to go to the gym after work, but you can't exercise in the morning because you're not a morning person. Hey, if you don't like one of these excuses, keep shopping. I'm sure you'll find one that fits.

Truth is, from time to time, we all make excuses for abandoning our dreams. I know I have. I remember accepting a job as a technical writer for the local phone company, even though my dream was to own my own business. But I came up with all kinds of excuses for taking the job.

"It's a regular paycheck," I rationalized.

"I'll get great medical benefits," I rationalized.

"I'll get two weeks' paid vacation," I rationalized.

"I'll save money by not having to buy office equipment," I rationalized.

"I'll have a better-looking resume for future jobs," I rationalized.

> Dreams are the seedlings of reality.
>
> –James Allen, author

I made a zillion excuses as to why I should abandon my dream and take a "secure" job. But the fact remained that I had no passion for technical writing. I was good at the writing part, but I was a lousy technician. The guy who hired me did me a big favor two months into the job. He fired me.

I'll be honest—I didn't like being fired. I was ashamed. Humiliated. Angry. I sulked around for two days, pacing the floor in the middle of the night. Then the third morning I got up, looked in the mirror and said, "Face it, you took a job you didn't like and weren't very good at for a paycheck. The guy who fired you did you both a favor—so get back to chasing your dream!"

And that's what I did. A year later I launched a successful publishing career. As for the guy who fired me, if I could remember his name, I'd send him a Christmas card every year. I've had periods in my publishing career where I earned more in a month than I could have earned in a year as a technical writer. Plus, I'm now working in a career I love, picking my own projects and setting my own hours, while producing books that help people grow personally and professionally. Hey, it doesn't get any better than that. And to think I owe it all to a "boss" who kicked me out of the corporate nest and forced me to fly in the direction of my dream.

## Are You a Climber, a Quitter, or a Camper?

Because we live in a dream-taking world, we're confronted with adversity all day, every day. Whether it's little nuisance adversities—

getting the kids to school on time. Or big life-altering adversities—a major illness, or worse, a sudden death in the family—we can't escape from adversity. And with each new adversity comes a new opportunity to buy an excuse rather than to sell yourself on your dreams.

For 15 years Paul Stoltz, a management consultant for Fortune 500 companies, has been studying adversity and its effect on workers and their job performance. Stoltz says that just as people's intelligence can be measured by IQ tests, so can their adversity quotient be measured by "AQ tests." Stoltz divides the workforce into three AQ groups: Climbers, Quitters, and Campers.

*Climbers* seek challenges.

*Quitters* flee from challenges.

And *Campers*, well, they just want to know what's for lunch.

Not surprisingly, Climbers don't blame others for setbacks, and they take responsibility for fixing problems. In other words, Climbers refuse to shop for excuses, and, as a result, Climbers are Dream Makers, making things happen and getting things done. Stoltz estimates 10% of workers are Climbers.

Quitters, on the other hand, flee from challenges. They have the "it's-not-my-job" mentality, and, like Dream Takers, Quitters are quick to make excuses and even quicker to blame others when things don't go as planned. Quitters make up the bottom 10% of the workforce.

Last (but certainly not least), there are the Campers, who constitute about 80% of a typical workforce. "What do most people do when the going gets tough?" Stoltz asks. "They camp!"

"[Most] people resist giving up their comforts, no matter what the price," Stoltz observes. Sounds a lot like Dream Fakers and Dream Undertakers, doesn't it—people who have dreams but bury them under a pile of excuses. (Interestingly, Stoltz says that because Climbers cause tension in the tent, Campers and Quitters often try to drive Climbers away.)

## The Good News Is You're a Born Dream Maker!

Now, here's the good news about your AQ. According to Stoltz, who has measured the AQ of more than 100,000 people, *we're all born climbers!* Which means that most campers—80% of the population who just want to huddle in the tent until the storm passes—can be reprogrammed to become climbers!

It seems that we're all hardwired at birth to trek to the summit, but, unfortunately, experience has taught us that it's a lot easier to stay inside the tent than to keep climbing when we encounter rough weather on the mountain of life. In other words, it's tempting for us to huddle with the other 80%-ers and warm our hands on a bonfire of excuses. Problem is, since we're all born climbers, and since it's every climber's dream to make it to the summit, we'll always feel unfulfilled until we extinguish our excuses and start trekking toward our dream again.

## Excuses—They're Everywhere, They're Everywhere!

Stoltz's research on AQ is important for two reasons. One, it proves that we're all born Dream Makers and that once people are made aware of their low AQ and taught strategies to better handle adversity, then they can get back on the road to making their dreams come true.

And two, Stoltz points out that as the world gets messier and more complicated, it's more important than ever that people learn how to raise their AQ. For the last 15 years, Stoltz has asked his clients to count the number of adverse events they experience in a given day—from little adversities like the mail being late to big adversities like embezzling by a key employee. Ten years ago the average number of adversities was seven per day. Five years ago it was 13. In 2000, it was 23—PER DAY! Stoltz says, "The trend for increasing adversities is global and independent of industry." Not very encouraging news for Dream Fakers and Undertakers, is it?

There's no getting around the fact that complexity breeds adversity. Five years ago, for example, you likely wouldn't have gotten stressed out if your Internet connection went bad. Why? Because less than 5% of the population even knew what the Internet was! But today, a major Internet disruption would affect millions of workers around the world. You add cell phones that get lost and DVD players that break to the equation, and you have adversities doubling every five years or so. If you think it's easy to shop for excuses today, just wait five years—you'll have a Sam's Club of excuses to shop at!

## Simple, But Not Easy

Strategy #5 for making your dreams come true *Shop for Shoes, Not Excuses*—is very simple to understand. But it's not easy to practice, that's for sure. It's like the syndicated *Pickles* cartoon by Brian Crane that I saw recently in the local paper. Mr. and Mrs. Pickles, an elderly couple, are sitting down to dinner with their young granddaughter, Gina.

"Do you like pickled beets?" Mrs. Pickles asks the girl.

"Yes, I love them," Gina replies.

"How many would you like?" Mrs. Pickles asks.

"None, thanks," the little girl replies.

"None?" says Mrs. Pickles."I thought you said you loved them."

"I love them in theory, but not on my plate," Gina says innocently.

*Strategy #5, Shop for Shoes, Not Excuses,* is a lot like this Pickles' cartoon—you may love your dreams in theory, but not on your plate. Why? Because our plates are piled so high with adversities that they smother our dreams! It's easy to give in to excuses because, well, they're everywhere! Excuses come in all shapes and sizes—big, small, simple, complex, sad, funny—and they're all so-o-o-o tempting! But excuses are like cigarettes. They're highly addictive, and they come in a pretty package with a bold warning label: *This excuse is hazardous to the health of your dreams!*

I'll close this chapter with an anonymous poem that sums up what kind of world we would be living in if all the Dream Makers suddenly settled for making excuses instead of making their dreams come true.

**It Can Be Done**

The man who misses all the fun,
Is he who says, "It can't be done."
In solemn pride he stands aloof,
And greets each venture with reproof.
Had he the power, he'd erase
The history of the human race!
We'd have no radio or motor cars,
No street lit by electric stars;
No telegraph, no telephone,
We'd linger in the age of stone.
The world would sleep if things were run,
By men who said, "It can't be done."

STRATEGY 6

# Feed the White Dog, Fence the Red Dog

*Work harder on yourself than you do at your job. When you work at your job, you make a living. When you work on yourself, you'll make a fortune.*

–Jim Rohn,
motivational speaker

A man sets up a meeting with his minister to discuss his constant inner struggles.

"It's like I have two dogs inside me fighting all the time," the man says. "The white dog is the good dog. He's fighting to be honest. To do the right thing. To be strong and not to give into temptations.

"The red dog is the opposite," the man continues. "The red dog is fighting to cut corners. To put myself above all others. To give in to temptations."

"Which dog usually wins?" the minister asks.

The man ponders the question before giving this memorable answer.

*"The dog that always wins is the one I say, 'Sic 'em!' to."*

Isn't that a great story? Doesn't it capture the inner struggles all of us face dozens of times every day, such as, "Do I eat one of those donuts someone brought to work today?" The red dog says, "Eat it!" The white dog says, "Stick to your diet." Or struggles like, "Do I get up and go to the early service at church before my golf game, or do I sleep in?" The red dog says, "You deserve the extra sleep!" The white dog says, "Go to church, for you have much to be thankful for."

And so goes the constant fights between the red dog and the white dog. Sometimes the red dog wins. Sometimes the white dog wins. But, in the end, the outcome of each fight is fixed, for *the winner is always the dog you choose to win!*

## Choices Determine Our Destiny

Now, you may be asking, "What do the red dog and the white dog have to do with living my dreams?" The answer is, "Everything!" You see, your choices make up the sum total of who you are and what you become. If you choose to let the red dog of over-eating beat the white dog of moderation 90% of the time, guess what you'll become? Overweight, out of shape, and unhappy about it. If you choose to let the red dog of procrastination beat the white dog of "do-it-ability," guess what you'll become? A do-nothing drowning in a sea of unfinished projects.

The good news is that you get to choose the winner of every battle. Unfortunately, the bad news is the same—you get to choose the winner of every battle! Which means you and only you are ultimately responsible for who you are and what you become in life.

As Stephen Covey, author of *The 7 Habits of Highly Effective People,* observes, "... there is a gap or space between stimulus and response, and the key to both our growth and happiness is how we use that space." In other words, between every stimulus and response, there is a pause. In that pause, we make our choices. And in those choices, we shape ourselves and our lives.

Likewise, every time your red dog and white dog are fighting, there is a pause before you say, "sic 'em." In that pause, you choose the winner. And, over time, you become the sum total of those choices. In effect, your choices determine your destiny. When all is said and done, Dream Makers live their dreams because they have the discipline and the self-awareness necessary to choose the white dog over the red dog most of the time.

## Get Out of Your Own Way!

In a dream-taking world, there are two major forces trying to take your dreams. The first kind is the outside world, which is what we've talked about for the first five strategies in this book.

The second dream-taking force is our inner world; that is, the fight between our red dog and our white dog. And more often than not, it's the inner world that keeps us from living our dreams. Multi-billionaire Warren Buffet, the most successful stock market investor in history, says that most fairly smart people could have what he has but, in his words, "They can't get out of their own way."

"Why do smart people do things that interfere with the output they're entitled to?" Buffet asks rhetorically. "It gets into the habits and character and temperament and behaving in a rational manner. Not getting in your own way."

> If you look at successful people from around the world, you notice a common element among them. They all have a dream of where they will fit in the future.
>
> –Willie Jolley, author

In essence, what Buffet is saying is that most people fail to become Dream Makers because they keep telling the red dog to "sic 'em" instead of the white dog. When people choose their dog based on their irrational emotions, instead of their rational intellect, they're likely to choose the red dog every time.

But let's face it, it's getting harder and harder to choose the white dog to win in a world that glorifies the red dog of instant gratification. High-fat junk food dominates the grocery store shelves. Credit cards are as easy to get as postage stamps. And with cable TV offering 200-plus channels, there's always something to watch on the boob tube.

Yet, in order to make our dreams come true, we have to keep choosing the white dog to win. That's why today, more than ever, it's crucial for people to understand and practice *Strategy #6: Feed the White Dog, Fence the Red Dog.* How do you do that? You begin by becoming aware of the red dogs in your life.

## Know Your Red Dogs

I think everyone can relate to the red dog vs. the white dog analogy. The particulars of our inner struggles may be different. But we all have our struggles, don't we? We know what is right and what's best for us. We know the white dog should win every fight. And we want the white dog to win—we really, *really* do!

But that red dog just won't leave us alone! And he's always rested and ready for battle, nourished by a full meal of excuses, rationalizations, and justifications. Here are just a few of his favorites:

"Everyone has one."

"One more won't hurt."

"I'll pay for it when I get my bonus."

"I deserve this...."

"I'll do it tomorrow."

"It's not worth the effort."

The worst part is, the more you feed the red dog, the hungrier he gets!

My point is this: We all have red dogs and white dogs, and they fight with each other all day long. The key to living our dreams is to reward our white dogs by feeding them, and to control our red dogs by starving them or fencing them in.

We all have red dogs. That's a given. But all too many people ignore their red dogs or mistake them for harmless pets, enabling the red dogs to dominate their decisions and run their lives.

Dream Makers, on the other hand, know their strengths and weaknesses. They know their red dogs by name. That's why Dream Makers are able to "get out of their own way," as Warren Buffet puts it. Dream Makers know where their red dogs sleep, and they take special care to choose the white dogs when a battle breaks out.

The first step in controlling our red dogs is to identify them. How about you—do you know your strengths and weaknesses? Can you identify your red dogs by name? Take a moment to list three to five red dogs in each category below. I've made a partial list of my red dogs as an example.

**My Personal Red Dogs**

| *Big Red Dogs* | *Small Red Dogs* |
| --- | --- |
| 1. Quick temper | 1. Sweet tooth |
| 2. Compulsive | 2. Impatient |
| 3. Quick to offer unsolicited advice | 3. Worry-wart |
| 4. | 4. |
| 5. | 5. |

**Your Personal Red Dogs**

| *Big Red Dogs* | *Small Red Dogs* |
| --- | --- |
| 1. ____________ | 1. ____________ |
| 2. ____________ | 2. ____________ |
| 3. ____________ | 3. ____________ |
| 4. ____________ | 4. ____________ |
| 5. ____________ | 5. ____________ |

Once you've named your red dogs, you've taken the first step to controlling them. Now let's look at the two basic ways you can take charge of your red dogs.

## Starve Your Red Dogs

There are two ways to control your red dogs. The first way is to starve them, which means you refuse to feed them excuses, rationalizations, and justifications that make them strong. The second way is to fence them in, which means you keep them away from yourself as much as you can. Let's look at the starving method first.

Starving your red dogs means refusing to give into temptations. This is the way most people try to control their red dogs. One problem. Most people lack discipline, and the red dogs are relentless! Which means that all too often, the strategy of starving your red dogs is doomed to failure.

> Never laugh at anyone's dream. People who don't have dreams don't have much.
>
> –Steve Price

For example, a couple of times a week, my co-workers bring in fresh donuts for the office. Oh, no... one of my small red dogs is a sweet tooth. As soon as I see those donuts, the red dog starts whispering in my ear: "*M-m-m-m, look at those fresh donuts. You had a small breakfast—go ahead and have one.*" If I resist the first time, the red dog is after me when I go back into the kitchen for more coffee: "*You were so-o-o-o strong the first time. Why don't you tear one of those donuts in half—that way you can remain strong and still have your donut.*"

As the day wears on, the red dog never lets up. "*Hey, you had a small lunch. You're got plenty of room for a donut. Besides, you're playing tennis tonight, and you'll run those calories off. Come on—what's one little donut? You don't want them to go stale, do you? Do you know how many children in this world go to bed hungry, and you're going to let these donuts go to waste? What are you, cold-hearted?*" I have to fight the sweet-tooth red dog all day long.

Meanwhile, my white dog is telling me to munch on the fresh carrot sticks in the refrigerator. I know the carrot sticks are good for me. I know they are high in fiber and low in fat. I know all the reasons I should choose the carrot sticks over the donut. But you know what—at least twice a week, I choose the red dog to win and grab a donut. I'm also 10 pounds overweight right now. No big mystery as to why, is there?

## Don't Keep Oreos in the Cupboard

The second way to control your red dogs is to keep them fenced in. By this I mean that you structure your life so that your red dogs have limited contact with your white dogs. Another name for this strategy is "Don't keep Oreos in the cupboard."

I call it that because I love Oreo cookies. So I learned a long time ago that the white dog doesn't have a chance if I keep Oreos in the house. You see, I don't eat Oreos one cookie at a time. I eat Oreos one row at a time—with milk! I've never had a package of Oreos last more than two days in my house. Never! So if I tried to keep Oreos in the house, I'd be setting myself up for failure. The red dog would be fat and happy, and I'd be fat and miserable.

So, I refuse to keep Oreos in the cupboard. In fact, I refuse to keep sweets in my house at all. No ice cream. No cookies. No candy bars. No Hershey's Kisses. I buy Girl Scout cookies every year because it's a great cause—and then I give them away! I've fenced in my house and made it a no-sweet zone. By fencing out my biggest temptations, I can "get out of my own way."

## Are You Feeding Your White Dog Enough?

What about you—do you know what your red dogs are? If so, are you trying to control them by starving them? If you're succeeding in controlling your red dogs by starving them, good for you! You're a person of exceptional discipline!

But if the starving method isn't working, I suggest you try fencing your red dogs. For example, overspending is a BIG red dog for many people in this country. That's why the average family carries more than $8,000 in credit card debt from month to month (at 20%, it's costing them $1,600 a year in interest fees!). They try to starve the red dog of impulsive buying, but when the red dog and white dog begin to fight, they can't resist saying "sic 'em" to the red dog. Meanwhile, the balance on the credit card never gets reduced, and another $1,600 a year goes into VISA's pocket instead of theirs.

So, I suggest you do what I do—just as I don't keep Oreos in the cupboard, don't keep credit cards in your wallet! Some people go to extraordinary lengths to fence in the red dog of credit-card spending—they cut their cards up! Hey, if that's what it takes to fence in your red dogs, I say grab the scissors and pass the credit cards!

Dream Makers control their red dogs by fencing them—but they don't stop there! They make it a point to nourish their white dogs by feeding them every chance they get! It's called positive reinforcement, and it's the most effective way to shape positive behavior. As Mark Twain once said, "An occasional compliment is necessary to keep up one's self-respect. When you cannot get a compliment any other way, pay yourself one."

I've learned that my white dogs thrive on compliments, so I don't hesitate to pet them when they win a battle. For example, when I feel my temper rising, but I manage to bite my tongue instead of lashing out, I compliment myself for showing maturity. When someone makes an innocent remark, and I manage to resist the temptation to make a sarcastic comment, I compliment myself for being considerate. If you compliment yourself every time your white dogs have a victory, I guarantee that you'll feel better about yourself and start pulling for your white dogs more often!

## Who Let the Dogs Out?

If you want to live your dreams, you have to get out of your own way by becoming your best ally, instead of your worst enemy. I'm not saying it's easy to control your red dogs. Old habits are hard to break, that's for sure.

It's like the *Peanuts* cartoon where Lucy and Charlie Brown are playing on the same baseball team, and, as always, they're in the process of losing the game. Lucy is playing the outfield and Charlie Brown is pitching. Lucy has just missed an easy fly ball, and she explains her error to Charlie Brown this way:

*"Sorry I missed the easy fly ball, manager. I thought I had it, but suddenly I remembered all the others I've missed. The past got in my eyes."*

"The past got in my eyes"—what a great line! And that's exactly what happens to Dream Fakers and Undertakers—their past gets in their eyes! So, by falling victim to old, unproductive patterns of behavior, they end up stealing their own dreams.

Bill Anton, the Director of the Counseling Center for Human Development at the University of South Florida, says this about people's efforts to break bad habits:

*"Don't underestimate the adversary, which is yourself."*

He's right, of course. Our inner red dogs are formidable opponents. But I'd add one sentence to Anton's observation:

*"Don't underestimate your ability to fence in the adversary and live your dreams."*

# STRATEGY 7

# Be an All Out, Not a Hold Out

*I've learned through the years that anyone who thinks earnestly and sincerely—and then does something about it—goes somewhere.*

–Dr. Norman Vincent Peale

Imagine for a moment that you're the mayor of a city of 70,000 people.

Now imagine that a man walks into your office carrying a beautiful hand-carved, brightly painted wooden carousel horse. The man tells you he will donate the horse and dozens of others, plus construct a working old-fashioned carousel *free of charge to the city* under one condition: The city agrees to donate the land and operate the carousel once it's completed.

Your astonishment turns to skepticism when you learn the man has no money for the project. He says he expects no money from the city. He has no special standing in the community. He has no experience in building carousels. Oh, and he works at a full-time job and can only dedicate four evenings a week to the project. All he has to begin the project are four painted carousel ponies in his garage and a big dream in his heart.

So, you're faced with making a decision—do you give this man the go-ahead? Or do you politely turn him down? You mull the decision over in your mind. You know it's an impossible task for one man. The project could cost hundreds of thousands of dollars and take years to complete. Let's face it—most people with a dream this big would fall off their cloud and quit once reality set in.

But there's something about this man that tells you he could pull off the impossible. You search his face, looking for a clue to the intangible quality that sets him apart, that indicates that this man has that rare quality that separates Dream Makers… from Dream Fakers.

What's that quality? *Commitment!* That's what you're looking for in the man—a burning, deep-seated commitment that will enable him to overcome obstacles and live his dream.

You look deep into the man's eyes and you can see the determination. You don't know what fuels his dream. You don't know where he gets his drive. All you know is *he's an all-out, not a hold-out.* So, what do you do? Do you give the man the green light to pursue his impossible dream?

## Green Light to Go for It!

If your name is Dan Kemmis and you're the mayor of Missoula, Montana, you give the carousel man, Chuck Kaparich, the go-ahead. You shake your head in amazement as he picks up his wooden horse and leaves the room. But something tells you that this guy will pull off the impossible.

*And he doesn't disappoint you!*

Amazingly, the more Chuck Kaparich carves, the more his dream grows. He envisions his horses spinning on a restored antique frame driven by an authentic steam engine and accompanied by a first-class pipe organ. And he dreams of housing the carousel in a new, open-air brick building sitting in Caras Park on the banks of the Clark Fork River surrounded by a wide-brick walk under a canopy of trees.

As Kaparich's dream grows, his commitment becomes contagious! Volunteers line up to help and contributions come pouring in. Within weeks the first wave of volunteers is cutting, carving, sanding, and painting the horses in Kaparich's garage, as a dozen retired craftsmen work in a drafty barn to restore an abandoned 80-year-old carousel frame and gears. Meanwhile, an organ repairman and a handful of workers start building America's largest carousel band organ.

> Your dreams can come true. I'm living proof of it. I left home at seventeen and had nothing but rejections for twenty-five years. I wrote more than twenty-five screen plays, but I never gave up.
>
> –Michael Blake,
> Academy Award winning author of
> *Dances with Wolves*

On Saturday, May 27, 1995, five years after the first meeting with the mayor of Missoula, Chuck Kaparich smiles broadly as dozens of children ride 38 prancing ponies and two charging chariots around and around the Carousel for Missoula. In the first summer alone, the carousel serves 125,000 riders and hosts 100 birthday parties, as well as dozens of receptions and two weddings.

## The Power of Commitment

Today the Carousel for Missoula is a lasting tribute to what can happen when one person has a big dream and an unshakable commitment to make it come true. By faithfully practicing *Strategy #7: Be an All Out, Not a Hold Out,* Chuck Kaparich doggedly assembled his dream one hand-carved piece at a time. This was no easy task, given that it took 400 to 800 hours to build just one horse!

But Kaparich wasn't focused on the *obstacles,* even though there were thousands of big and small obstacles to overcome. No, Kaparich focused on the *outcome*—from day one, he could see a whirling, hand-built carousel in his mind's eye. As a result of his commitment, his dream became more real than the reality of the project, and it was just a matter of time before Chuck Kaparich became another Dream Maker in a dream-taking world.

What is this concept we call "commitment," and why is it so crucial to making our dreams come true? The dictionary defines commitment as "a pledge or promise to do something." This definition is fine for a dictionary, I suppose. But the dictionary definition doesn't do justice to the depth and passion of a Dream Maker's commitment. As I see it, to become a Dream Maker in a dream-taking world, you need the three "Ds" of commitment:

1. Drive
2. Discipline
3. "Do it"-ability

Rather than talk about each of these in depth, I'd like to tell you about some Dream Makers who best exemplify these characteristics so that you can see the three "Ds" in action.

## 1) Drive: The Fire Within

Let's start by talking about the internal combustion engine that all Dream-Makers possess—**drive.** A Dream-Maker who personifies drive is Jimmy Shea, who was perhaps the most inspiring Dream Making story in the 2002 Winter Olympics held in Salt Lake City, Utah.

Shea was the first competitor to become a third-generation Olympian—his grandfather, Jack, had won two speed skating medals at the 1932 games, and his father, Jim, Sr., had competed in cross country skiing in the 1964 Olympics.

The story of Jim, Jr. sounds more like a made-for-TV movie than a true story, but true it is—and his quest to represent his family as a third-generation Olympian is a testimony to one man's drive to fulfill a family dream.

Jimmy Shea chose to compete in a made-for-maniacs sport called "skeleton." The name is fitting, for the contestants literally risk their lives as they hurtle around an ice-packed bobsled course face down on a small sled at speeds up to 60 miles per hour with their chins only two inches from the ice. Obviously, skeleton competitors aren't short on courage. But what separated Jim Shea from the other competitors was his drive to compete, no matter what price he had to pay.

Prior to the Olympics, Shea was mostly a minor league performer in the sport of skeleton. But what he lacked in experience and know-how, he made up for in his competitive drive. For five years he competed on the European circuit, barely winning enough prize money to stay alive. He lived off hot dogs and bread, and hitchhiked from event to event, sleeping in unheated bobsled sheds and cow barns.

When his money ran out, he called his father and told him to sell his jeep for whatever he could get. Jim, Sr., sold it for $1,200 and kicked in some of his own money so his son could keep competing. Jim, Jr.'s drive resulted in his not only making the U.S. Olympic team, *but he went on to win a gold medal on his very last run!*

Sadly, the win was bittersweet, for 17 days before the games began, the grandfather, 91-year-old Jack Shea, was killed in a car accident. But Jim, Jr. used the tragedy to further fuel his drive by placing a photograph of his grandfather inside his helmet. As Jim, Jr. tearfully embraced his father after his winning run, he removed his grandfather's photo from his helmet and waved it wildly to the crowd as 13,000 spectators chanted in unison, *"U-S-Shea! U-S-Shea! U-S-Shea!"*

Jimmy Shea proved that the key to willpower is *wantpower*—if you want something bad enough, if your inner fire burns hot enough, you'll find a way to make it happen.

## 2) Discipline: Concentrated Commitment

The second essential ingredient in commitment is **discipline.** I call discipline "concentrated commitment" because it's like concentrated orange juice—reduced to its very essence. Discipline is the laser-like focus that empowers you to ignore all the counterproductive distractions and stay on a direct course to your dream.

My selection for the person who most embodies discipline is a little man, only five-foot, one-inch-tall and 117 pounds. But he has a muscular build, so it's very easy for him to put on weight. One problem—he's a jockey, so putting on weight is not an option in his career.

The man's name is Laffit Pincay, and because of his unswerving discipline, he's become the winningest jockey in horse-racing history—more than 9,000 races won and still counting, even though he's 55 years old! How does he keep so trim at an age when most men are fighting a losing battle against the dreaded "mid-life bulge"? Discipline!

> Rose-colored glasses are never made in bifocals. Nobody wants to read the small print in dreams.
>
> –Ann Landers

You see, ever since Pincay started riding at 17 years of age, he has controlled his weight by consuming only 850 calories a day, and he's maintained that regimen for almost 40 years! Considering that the average American consumes 2,100 calories a day, Pincay is voluntarily eating two-and-one-half times less food than you or I. When a reporter asked Pincay the last time he treated himself to a piece of cake or ice cream, he didn't hesitate with an answer.

"Never," he replied.

Now, I know that some of you are thinking that Pincay's level of discipline just isn't worth it—that people like him are missing out on many of life's little pleasures. That may be true, but all I know is this. Because of discipline, Laffit Pincay is living *his* dream. So, I suggest you ask yourself two questions: "Am I living *my* dream? If I had Pincay's discipline, would I be living my dream?" I think we both know the answer to that one.

I'm not saying that you need to live a monk-like existence in order to live your dreams. But I am saying that discipline is key to making your dreams come true. Just think if everyone had half of Pincay's discipline. Or even one-fourth. Most likely, they'd be Dream Makers, instead of Dream Fakers and Undertakers.

Let's face it, everybody wants to be Michael Jordan. But nobody wants to run wind sprints. Problem is, you can't have one without the other. You can't have success without discipline. An American minister named Harry Emerson Fosdick captured the power of discipline in this brief poem:

*No horse gets anywhere 'til he is harnessed.*

*No steam or gas ever drives anything until it is confined.*

*No Niagara Falls is ever turned into light and power*
*until it is tunneled.*

*No life ever grows great until it is focused, dedicated,*
*and disciplined.*

In the end, you have a choice. You can exercise discipline and live your dreams. Or you can give into immediate gratification and watch in exasperation as your dreams go up in smoke. Dream Makers opt for discipline. What about you?

## 3) "Do-It"-ability: Purposeful, Productive Action

As for the third "D" of commitment, **"do-it"-ability,** don't bother looking it up in the dictionary—I made this term up. (Big surprise, eh?).

Do-it-ability goes by several different names, including the words "action" and "work." But the reason I chose do-it-ability to describe Dream Makers' activities is because lots of people perform actions. And lots of people work hard. But that doesn't mean those actions are helping turn a worthwhile dream into reality. As Burke Hedges always says, *"Don't confuse activity with productivity."* Boy, is that the truth!

We all know people at work who are as busy as bees. They draft memos. They attend meetings. They organize their desks. They update their Palm Pilots. They load new software into their computers. They attend training classes. But at the end of the day, all of their actions don't do a thing to improve the company's bottom line! What a waste!

People with do-it-ability, on the other hand, *do what needs to be done* to turn productive, worthwhile dreams into reality. Rather than spend an hour cleaning off a messy desk, they use that hour to contact clients or follow up on prospects. As Albert Einstein said when a colleague made fun of his cluttered desk, "If a cluttered desk is the sign of a cluttered mind, what is an empty desk the sign of?"

I'd like to tell two stories that illustrate what do-it-ability *is not*... and what it *is*.

The first story is about Donald Gorske, a 47-year-old prison guard in Fond du Lac, Wisconsin. Gorske's dream was to be listed in the *Guinness Book of World Records*. He was committed to making his dream come true, that's for sure. And he showed extraordinary discipline. But you'd have to question how productive his actions were. You see, Gorske has eaten at least two Big Mac hamburgers every day for 29 years. All told, he has wolfed down 18,000 hamburgers, ensuring his place in the record book.

Now, there's no question that Gorske was committed to his dream. His daily actions were disciplined and purposeful. But productive? Worthwhile? Not in my book, unless you call clogging your arteries up being a productive, worthwhile endeavor.

The second story is about George Dawson, a man who grew up so poor that he was forced to drop out of school at age eight to work. As a result, he never learned to read or write. He worked as a laborer for seven decades, finally retiring from his own gardening business at 88. But Dawson wasn't ready to retire his dreams. He says he got tired of writing his name with an "X," so at age 98, he enrolled in an adult-education program in Dallas.

"I figured if I could lay a railroad tie as well as any man, and cook as well as any woman, I could learn to read as well as anyone else," Dawson said.

Now, it takes a lot of courage for a 98-year-old to attend school five days a week to learn a skill that most people have learned by the second grade. But what makes George Dawson's story even more remarkable is that at age 102, Dawson wrote his autobiography, *Life Is So Good!*

George Dawson is a living example of do-it-ability, that's for sure. He was committed to seeing a worthwhile dream come true, and, as a result, his actions were purposeful and productive—not to mention inspiring.

## Actions Speak Louder Than Words

I'd say that Jimmy Shea, Laffite Pincay, and George Dawson are shining examples of Dream Makers in a dream-taking world. Because they embraced *Strategy #7: Be an All Out, Not a Hold Out!*, they're living their dreams. While others talked about their drive, discipline, and do-it-ability, these three men were working on making their dreams come true.

I'll close with one final story that epitomizes what it means to be an all-out, not a hold-out. In the late 1800s, Rev. D.L. Moody, for whom the world-famous Moody Bible Institute is named, was crossing the ocean on a small ship when a storm hit. The 20-foot waves swept over the sides of the boat, flooding the hull. Moody ran down to help work the pumps. Several terrified passengers spotted Moody and asked him to pray for the ship's safety.

"*You pray while I pump!*" Moody replied.

Moody's classic response is often quoted from the pulpit by ministers who want to emphasize a key Biblical principle: *God provides the seeds, but we still have to plant them!*

In the end, there's no substitute for commitment. And commitment means rolling up your sleeves and making your dreams happen, no matter how dire the situation or how big the obstacles.

STRATEGY 8

# Don't Float Like a Feather When You Can Fly Like a Falcon

*To fulfill a dream, to be allowed to sweat over lonely labor, to be given the chance to create, is the meat and potatoes of life.*

–Bette Davis,
legendary movie star

It had been two months since the stroke—two long months filled with depression and self pity.

The man who had once dazzled movie audiences with his matinee-idol good looks and tough-guy swagger pulled himself out of bed. He leaned against the bathroom vanity and studied himself in the mirror. His top right lip drooped. His once muscled arms were withered and pasty white from lying in bed all day. He tried to make a wisecrack to the pitiful image in the mirror, but the syllables came out jumbled and slurred.

"*Your speech therapist is here—get to work!*" his wife barked.

The man—legendary actor Kirk Douglas—wiped away his tears, pulled back his shoulders, and shuffled out to meet the person who would teach him to talk again—at age 80!

Douglas faced months of tedious exercises to loosen his frozen lips, tongue, and cheeks. At 80, most people would resign themselves to living their final days in silence. But Douglas was a life-long Dream Maker. And he was a fighter—just like the roles he played in his most famous movies: A boxer in *The Champion.* A rebellious slave in *Spartacus.* A gunfighter in *Gunfight at the O.K. Corral.*

> No dream is too high for those with their eyes in the sky.
>
> –Buzz Aldrin,
> Apollo 11 astronaut

In 1996, at age 80, Douglas' dream was to accept the Lifetime Achievement Oscar he was to receive at the Academy Awards. He dreamed of walking on stage and giving an acceptance speech to millions of TV viewers worldwide. But the reality was the event was only four months away, and Douglas was unable to speak! Fueled by his dream, he pushed past his depression and worked for hours each day practicing "oral aerobics." Gradually, his speech improved from thick-tongued gibberish to slow, slurred sentences.

On Oscar night, Steven Spielberg introduced Kirk Douglas to a thunderous ovation. He waved to his four sons and to Anne, his wife of 47 years. Then he turned to the audience, and, remembering his speech therapists' instructions to pause... breathe... swallow... and articulate—he spoke these words:

"I see my four sons. They're proud of the old man. Anne, this belongs to you. I love you. Thank you for 50 wonderful years in the wonderful world of moviemaking."

The crowd understood every word, and they cheered and cried as Douglas ambled off the stage. Two years later, his recovery was so successful that he accepted a leading role in *Diamonds*, a movie about a retired boxer co-starring Lauren Bacall.

## Against the Wind

Kirk Douglas understands what it takes to become a Dream Maker in a dream-taking world. By practicing *Strategy #8: Don't Float Like a Feather When You Can Fly Like a Falcon,* Douglas overcame the obstacle of a stroke and has lived two late-life dreams.

When Douglas was hit by a stroke, he could have resigned himself to floating on the ill wind of misfortune like a feather. He could have easily resigned himself to defeat, giving in to self pity and playing the victim. But Douglas chose to fight against the wind, and, as a result, he soared above his affliction. Here are Douglas's words from his autobiography, *My Stroke of Luck:*

"One of the worst things about having a stroke is that people feel sorry for you. And since you feel sorry for yourself, you let them. Beware such temptation! Cling to your willpower—you need every ounce of it to get better. I had to take control. I had to will myself to get better. I had to fight for it!"

Yes, it's easier to float like a feather on the wind than to fly against it. But Dream Makers like Kirk Douglas understand that, in the end, it's not the wind that controls our destiny. It's our decision to *float with it...* or *fight against it...* that controls our destiny.

In Douglas' case, the wind was a stroke.

But the wind can take many forms.

Sometimes it's the *wind of reality:* Illnesses. Accidents. Family tragedies.

Sometimes it's the *wind of other people:* Oppression. Discrimination. Ignorance.

And sometimes it's the *wind of ourselves:* Bad habits. Anger. Fear.

Let's take a moment to discuss each of the three kinds of winds—reality, other people, and ourselves—and see how some Dream Makers manage to rise above the turbulence.

## Flying Into the Wind of Reality

Sixteen-year-old Mallory Code is one of the best junior golfers in the country. At 15, she won the Rolex Tournament of Champions, one of junior golf's majors. It was at the Rolex that thousands of TV viewers fell in love with her great attitude and mega-watt smile. It was also at the Rolex that TV cameras caught Mallory giving herself insulin during the final round.

You see, Mallory is diabetic. Yes, the diabetes is a nuisance. But it can be controlled. She wears an insulin pump on and off the golf course to regulate her insulin.

But she's also been diagnosed with cystic fibrosis. It can be controlled for a while. She takes 40 pills a day to replace the enzymes she lacks. And for a half hour each day, she wears a mechanical vest that beats her back to loosen the mucus in her lungs. But these are all temporary measures, for there's no cure for CF. If Mallory is one of the lucky ones, she may live into her 40s. Truth is, most children with CF die before they're out of their teenage years.

Mallory is flying into the cold wind of reality, and she knows it. She'd never think of floating along—she's too competitive. Too strong willed. And has too much to live for. She knows CF is a death sentence, but she refuses to feel sorry for herself. And don't you dare feel sorry for her, either. She hates that!

"My life is perfect in almost every way," Mallory said during an interview with Martin Fennelly of the *Tampa Tribune*. "I've got this awesome family, awesome friends, and awesome relationship with the Lord Jesus. I've got golf, dance, everything. I don't want to be the little sick girl out there."

Mallory is a Dream Maker because she dwells on her *life sentence*, not her death sentence. She knows she's been dealt a bad hand. But she knows that life is like poker—there are 2,598,960 possible five-card poker hands, and we're all dealt just one. The beauty of it is, you *don't have to have the best hand to win!* And on the golf course and in life—Mallory Code is a winner!

## Flying Into the Wind of Other People

There are no expiration dates on some people's dreams. Just ask Charlie "Two Shoes" Tsui. It took Tsui 55 years to see his dream come true. Here's his story:

WWII was just winding down when the 10-year-old Tsui met some U.S. Marines who had been assigned to protect Tsangkou Air Base near the boy's village in northern China. The Marines befriended Tsui, and he brought them boiled eggs and warm peanuts his mother cooked. The Marines taught him English and nicknamed him Charlie "Two Shoes" because they couldn't pronounce his name.

In 1949, the Marines pulled out and Mao's Red Army took control of the area. The wind shifted from the free wind of capitalism to the oppressive wind of communism, and when Tsui refused to renounce the United States, the communists locked him in prison for seven years, and he spent another 10 years under house arrest.

But Tsui was a Dream Maker, and his dream was to become a U.S. citizen, no matter how long it took. Decades passed, and when tensions between the U.S. and China settled down, Tsui wrote letters to some of the Marines he'd met and started his long quest to become an American.

On Saturday, July 1, 2000, wearing the same Marine Corps dress pants the Marines had given him as a boy, Tsui walked onto the lawn at Ft. Johnston in Southport, North Carolina, for the swearing-in ceremony to become an American citizen. Tsui's amazing journey to fulfill his 55-year-old dream is one of my favorite stories about flying like a falcon into a headwind of other people's freedom-sapping dogmas.

## Fed-Ex to Freedom

Dream Makers aren't immune to oppression and prejudice any more than anyone else. But Dream Makers find a way to prevail. In the case of Charlie "Two Shoes," he persevered for decades until his dream came true. In the case of Henry "Box" Brown, he combined courage and creativity to turn his dreams into reality. Here is his story:

Henry Brown was born into slavery in Richmond, Virginia, and, as was the case with all slaves, he did his best to maintain his dignity in the face of daily incivilities and humiliations. But in 1848, Brown suffered the ultimate emotional trauma—his wife and children were sold to a slave owner who was moving out of state. Henry was devastated!

But Brown was a Dream Maker, and he decided that rather than give in to his anger and suffering, he would use it as fuel to drive his dream of freedom for himself and his family. So, Brown came up with an ingenious escape plan. With the help of a white friend, Brown built a padded wooden crate and had himself shipped to abolitionists in Philadelphia!

For 26 hours Brown traveled as cargo, often upside down, until he arrived safe in the fold of antislavery leaders, who nicknamed him "Box" Brown. By lecturing at abolitionist events throughout the North, Brown earned enough money to buy the freedom of his wife and children. Henry's immediate family weren't the only ones affected by his dream-making determination—*in the summer of 2002, dozens of descendants of Henry "Box" Brown plan to celebrate their 132nd family reunion!*

The wind of oppression, intolerance, or just plain evil intent still whirls around the globe like a tornado. But Dream Makers like Charlie "Two Shoes" Tsui and Henry "Box" Brown fly into the eye of the storm, protected only by the passion of their dreams. By way of wit, courage, and determination, these Dream Makers managed to make their dreams come true, despite tremendous hardships and overwhelming odds.

## Flying Into the Wind of Ourselves

The last wind I want to talk about is the wind of ourselves; that is, the internal, self-destructive wind that holds us back from living up to our full potential. We touched on this in the last chapter when we talked about triumphing over our inner conflicts by "fencing your red dogs."

But flying into the wind of ourselves refers to what Dream Makers must do once their red dogs are already on the loose. These Dream Makers may have been bitten by bad habits, such as addiction... or bad circumstances, such as abandonment or abuse as a child. But they somehow manage to escape the rabid jaws of self-destruction and fly toward their dreams.

Recently I read an article in the local paper about a 29-year-old woman whose dream was to escape the jaws of addiction once and for all. The woman had been abusing cocaine since she was 16. In 1996, she was arrested on coke possession charges and wound up in jail for three months. During that time, she had limited access to her two sons, the younger of whom was only two. But she had a lot of time to think about her choices over the last decade. And the more she thought, the more she was motivated to change. She enrolled in a program called SAMI, short for Substance Abusing Mothers and their Infants. Gradually, she started healing her wings and began the arduous journey of flying into the tortuous wind of self-examination:

> Cherish your dreams, for they are the children of your soul, the blueprint of your ultimate achievement.
>
> –Napoleon Hill, author

*"Jail will either slap you smart or slap you stupid," she said. "It slapped me smart in a big way."*

Now, here was a woman who had to overcome a decade of bad choices. But she had the good sense to recognize her bad patterns of behavior and to seek professional help that would empower her to make better choices in the future. On the date the article was written, she was reunited with her children and had been clean for 14 months.

I don't know what this woman's childhood was like for her to start abusing cocaine at 16, but rest assured there's a Dream Maker somewhere in this world who had to fly into a wind just as forceful as hers. Yes, a bad childhood is certainly a huge obstacle to overcome. But it doesn't have to be a script for self-destruction.

## Slapped Smart? Or Slapped Stupid?

I've thought a lot about the young woman's words, "Jail will either slap you smart or slap you stupid." But when you think about it, you realize she's not just talking about herself. In truth, her words ring true for all of us, because we all get slapped by our bad choices.

We all make poor choices from time to time, Dream Makers included. And Dream Makers get slapped for their poor choices, just like everyone else. But Dream Makers get slapped smart, not stupid! They pay attention to the slap and use it as a warning to change their behavior. Losers, on the other hand, just keep ignoring the slaps.

President George W. Bush, for example, got slapped smart one morning when he was 40 years old. George W is an outgoing guy who loves people and parties. One morning after a night of heavy drinking, he woke up with yet another hangover. He'd had lots of hangovers in his life, but for some reason, that hangover slapped him smart, instead of stupid. That morning, he decided to quit drinking.

It's been 14 years since George W took his last drink of alcohol. If he had let the hangover slap him stupid and continued to drink, odds are he never would have become president of the United States.

## What About You?

What about you—have you been slapped lately?

Maybe you were slapped when your out-of-shape neighbor suffered a heart attack.

Maybe you were slapped when one of your children asked you to quit smoking.

Maybe you were slapped when your company started laying off workers.

Maybe you were slapped when your nice boss was replaced by a jerk.

Maybe you were slapped when you had to loosen your belt another notch.

Maybe you were slapped when your credit card got rejected—again.

Maybe you were slapped when your teenager came home drunk or stoned.

Maybe you were slapped when your spouse said, "We've gotta talk...."

The point is this: We all get slapped by life from time to time. Think of these slaps as wake up calls, designed to get our attention. But Dream Makers *get slapped smart* and change their counter-productive behavior. Dream Fakers and Undertakers, on the other hand, *get slapped stupid* and keep repeating the same negative behaviors that have prevented them from living their dreams.

The only way to conquer yourself is to recognize the slaps for what they are—warning signs that some of your behavior patterns are working against your dreams.

As Sir Edmund Hillary, the first man to climb Mt. Everest noted, "It's not the mountain we conquer, but ourselves."

STRATEGY 9

# Know the Difference Between Good Debt, Bad Debt, and Dream Debt

*Debt works night and day, in fair weather and in foul. It gnaws at a man's substance with invisible teeth.*

–Henry Ward Beecher,
19th century minister

I sat in the dentist's chair, marveling at the brand new, hi-tech equipment surrounding me. When my dentist arrived, I congratulated her on her beautiful new office. But I couldn't resist a teasing comment.

"When I look around your office, one word keeps popping into my head," I said.

"What word is that?" she smiled.

"Debt," I replied. "All this new equipment must have cost a fortune."

"Yes," she laughed. "There's a lot of debt here. *But it's Good Debt.*"

My dentist is right—there is such a thing as "Good Debt." Her debt is Good Debt because the new equipment enables her to give her patients better care and to grow her business. My dentist may have had to borrow several hundred thousand dollars, but she's not worried. She knows the income her practice will generate in the coming months and years, plus the value of her growing list of patients, will far exceed her monthly loan payments. And once the loan is paid off, she'll not only own all the equipment, she'll be able to put the money from those retired loan payments into her pocket.

That's Good Debt, any way you look at it.

## Three Kinds of Debt

As I see it, Good Debt is just one of three types of debt. The other two are Bad Debt and something I call "Dream Debt." In this chapter, I'm going to concentrate on Dream Debt. But before I tell you what Dream Debt is and why it's so important, I'd like to talk briefly about Good Debt and Bad Debt.

First, let's start by defining debt. According to my Webster's dictionary, debt is *"an obligation to pay or return something."* I define Good Debt as any debt that enables you to grow your net worth, either *personally* (growing your skills and knowledge) or *financially* (growing your savings, assets, and equity).

My dentist's debt is Good Debt because it enables her to grow her business and make a profit while paying off the debt. Other examples of Good Debt are mortgages on your home or income-producing real estate, such as office buildings or apartment complexes.

Several years ago, for example, I owned three apartment buildings with mortgages totaling half a million dollars. *That's a lot of debt!* But today, 15 years later, the mortgages are retired and, through appreciation, the properties are now worth a million dollars. Good Debt enabled me to add a million dollars to my net worth in 15 years.

Taking out a loan to start or buy a profitable business is another example of Good Debt, as is taking out a loan to attend college or trade school, whereby you can increase your value in the marketplace. All of these debts are Good Debts because, managed correctly, they increase your net worth. With Good Debt, you own things that increase in value. Therefore, once the debt is retired, you're way ahead of the game.

## Bad Debt Is a Hangman's Noose

Bad Debt, on the other hand, is debt that reduces your net worth. Credit card debt is a classic example of Bad Debt. With credit card debt, a bank advances you money at 18% so you can buy stuff *today* that depreciates in value *tomorrow*. No one would even consider agreeing to a bank loan with 18% interest—yet that's what people who carry a credit card balance from one month to the next are doing. It's insane!

Credit card debt exploits the "buy now, pay later" mentality, which, unfortunately, is all too common today. Consider this: The average American family owes $8,000 in credit card debt. If a family made the minimum monthly payment of $130 on $8,000 of credit card debt at 18%, *it would take 47 years to retire the loan—plus, the payments would total more than $73,000, which is more than nine times the original amount!*

In the case of the Bad Debt of credit cards, *you don't own things—they own you*—because you have to keep paying for stuff years after you bring it home. Even if you bought, say, a DVD player on sale with your credit card, if you're like most people, by the time you get around to paying off your credit card balance, that DVD player will have cost three, four, five times its full retail price—PLUS, it will have depreciated in value! Dumb, dumb, dumb!

Bad debt is a hangman's noose that slowly strangles your net worth. Now are you beginning to see why Dream Makers follow *Strategy #9: Know the Difference Between Good Debt, Bad Debt, and Dream Debt?*

## Dream Debt

Now it's time to talk about the third kind of debt—Dream Debt. You've no doubt heard the expression, "a debt of gratitude." Well, that's the essence of Dream Debt—an obligation to repay your debt of gratitude to all of the people who gave you a leg up in this world. People like your parents. Your grandparents. Good friends who stood beside you in tough times. Teachers and coaches who mentored you. And veterans who fought and died so that you could remain free.

Dream Debt reminds us that we weren't born in a vacuum, that we're a complex combination of inherited genes... God-given talents and abilities... shared values... cultural mores... family history... personal experience... and national identity. And, as is the case with any debt, we OWE a debt of gratitude to the people who helped shape our dreams, as well as to the people whose dreams shaped our world.

The best way to explain Dream Debt is to briefly recount my family history. Although my family history will differ from yours in the details, it's the same in one very important respect: Your family tree is replete with stories of men and women whose dreams, courage, and sacrifices carved the steps of freedom and opportunity that you walk on today. What follows is just one of the thousands of stories that constitute my Dream Debt.

## Escape to America

In1841, 14-year-old John Buck of Leicestershire County in central England, stowed away on a ship bound for New York. During the long voyage he became acquainted with Thurzeah Ruckman, and several years later they married, eventually homesteading in Indiana where they raised nine children.

Twenty-five years later, in 1866, Evan Price of Romney, Wales, scraped up the money to emigrate to America. Evan's father was a destitute coal miner, so Evan had to raise the money on his own. Maybe he won a local lottery. Maybe he indentured himself, agreeing to work for room and board for seven years in exchange for passage to America. I don't know the specifics, but I do know Dream Makers find a way to live their dreams, and Evan's dream was to emigrate to America. So, 17-year-old Evan, his wife, and their one-year-old son sailed from England to America to start a new life.

In 1918, John Buck's great-granddaughter, Edna Buck, married Mark Price, the grandson of Evan Price. Mark and Edna had seven children during their 20-plus year marriage, one of whom was my father, Ernest Price.

The American branch of the Price family tree grew out of the desperate attempts by Evan Price and John Buck to escape the suffocating coal mines that snaked under the English landscape like shallow graves. Ironically, both men settled in rural Indiana, where the only steady job was—irony of ironies, coal mining.

## Dreams of a Better Life for Their Children

For at least five generations, the male ancestors on the Price side of my family tree coughed their lives away in the black caves of the coal mines. I'm sure on their lunch breaks in the mines, they dreamed of toiling in wide, sun-drenched fields. I'm sure they dreamed of working in cool, saltwater breezes. But in the 1800s, uneducated men living in rural Indiana and small English villages had few options outside the mines. So, for 150 years, dozens of Prices and Bucks pushed their dreams down a mine shaft, where they were smothered by a black blanket of coal dust.

I can't say coal mining in America was any easier than coal mining in England—mining in the 1800s was a dangerous, dirty, dead-end job, no matter where you worked. But at least in America, there was hope for a better life for your children. And that's what Evan Price and John Buck and every other immigrant who ever coughed their way through the black dust of the coal mines dreamed of—a better life for their children.

## Ernest Price Breaks the Coal Mining Cycle

My grandfather, Mark Price, was the last of the Prices to slave in the black tunnels of the coal mines, but his dark days were brightened by the dream that his only son and my father, "Ernie," would some day become a professional baseball player.

"I'd rather have my son play in the major leagues than become president of the United States," my grandfather would often say.

My dad was a good pitcher by local standards, but he lacked the talent to become a major leaguer. To complicate matters, he had the bad fortune to graduate from high school just as the Great Depression hit its stride. My dad applied for work in the mines, but they were laying off, not hiring. Even in the best of times, the local economy was depressed. But in the 1930s, most families in rural Indiana lived hand to mouth—my father wore the same pair of shoes every day for five years. My mother owned two dresses the entire time she was in high school.

In 1941, fate intervened to unlock the handcuffs that had shackled the Prices to the coal mines for 150 years. On December 7, 1941, the Japanese attacked Pearl Harbor, and my 28-year-old, unemployed father enlisted in the Army Air Corps. Shortly after basic training, Ernie Price and his bride of one year, Mary Riley, daughter of a Baptist preacher, headed to San Antonio, Texas, where my father was stationed for much of the war.

While in the service, my father took a machine shop class, and within months, he was teaching machine shop to new enlistees. After the war, my father's new-found skill as a machinist meant he had no need to return to the mines. For the next 32 years, my father worked as a machine shop instructor and technical writer with the Civil Service until his retirement at age 63.

## Getting Deeper in Dream Debt

My parents told me lots of stories about growing up during the Great Depression: Picking buckets of blackberries to sell in town. Swimming in the abandoned coal pits. Milking a contrary old cow at 5 a.m. in a snowstorm. Playing baseball against the local prison team. Coon hunting by moonlight.

As I look back, I realize my mom and dad were more embarrassed than embittered about growing up poor. I know it sounds crazy, but I think they blamed themselves for the humiliating poverty they endured as children.

The Depression hammered down my parents' spirits and nailed a low ceiling on their expectations. As a result, my dad was glad to have a steady job, even if it was a job he hated in his later years. Like most Depression-era people, my dad's dream was to have a secure job and a regular paycheck. Whether he liked the job or not was beside the point. For someone who grew up penniless and never had a full-time job until age 28, security was everything. And let's face it, a U.S. government job in the 1950s and '60s was about as secure as any job in the world.

Like a blacksmith's hammer on hot steel, the Depression permanently shaped my parents' lives. Even after the Depression was over, *my parents never got over the Depression!* When they left Indiana in their 20s, they left poverty behind. But for the rest of their lives, the memory of poverty followed my parents around like a family ghost, whispering to them to cling to their money like a shipwrecked sailor clings to a life raft. So, my parents counted their pennies. They bought a modest home. They bought used furniture and appliances. They drove used cars. They ate all their meals at home. And they set aside a portion of every paycheck to pay for my college education.

The Great Depression shrunk the size of my parents' personal dreams. They were too bludgeoned by their hard-scrabble childhood to dream of getting a college education for themselves. As a child, I remember asking my father if he'd ever gone to college, and his answer was always the same:

"I went to college, all right. The College of Hard Knocks," he'd laugh.

My parents, however, always assumed that I'd go to college. From the time I was old enough to talk, many of the conversations with my mother would begin, "When you go to college...."

In the summer of 1968, when I walked across the stage to receive my diploma from Illinois State University, I was the first member of the Price family to graduate from college. I was pretty proud of myself on graduation day. But you should have seen my parents—they were bursting with pride! *Their son—a college graduate!*

## What's Your Dream Debt?

That's basically the story of my Dream Debt—and it gets bigger with every blessing I receive. I'm forever indebted to my parents for the sacrifices they made on my behalf.

My story is just one of millions of stories woven into the cultural blanket that we call the American Dream. But today, the American Dream could just as easily be the Global Dream, because every person in every free nation in the world owes a Dream Debt to the people who made sacrifices for the generations that followed.

> They can't tax your dreams.
>
> –ad for American Express

When you get a chance, ask your parents to help you tally up your Dream Debt by recalling some of your family history. I guarantee you'll hear stories of great-grandparents who made courageous decisions… of widowed mothers who worked two jobs to support their families… of determined farmers who battled dust bowls and droughts… of brave soldiers who died on the battlefields of Gettysburg or on the beaches of Normandy.

*You owe them a huge Dream Debt!*

You may have had a brave ancestor emigrate alone from Italy to America, unable to speak the language, working from sunup to sundown, saving every penny to buy passage to America for his wife and children… then his parents… then his brothers and sisters… then his cousins.

*You owe him a huge Dream Debt!*

You may be descended from a young Irish woman who traveled to this country in steerage, only to be scorned by second-generation immigrants upon her arrival, denied jobs, packed into a shanty town and forced to take the jobs the other immigrants turned down.

*You owe her a huge Dream Debt!*

Your may be descended from Russian Jews who escaped their burning village torched by saber-wielding Cossack troops, arriving at Ellis Island in rags, unable to speak the language, and instantly immersed in a culture that mocked their appearance and derided their long-held customs.

*You owe them a huge dream debt!*

You may be descended from African slaves who bore with dignity the brutality of slavery and injustices of Jim Crow laws.

Or you may be descended from Native Americans who survived hundred-mile death marches to new reservations.

Or you may be descended from Chinese laborers who were shanghaied to Hawaii and forced to work as slaves in giant pineapple plantations.

Or you may be descended from penniless student-protesters who fled from Russian tanks during the 1956 Hungarian uprising.

Every story in every Dream Debt is unique. Every story in your Dream Debt is fascinating. And every story adds a bit more to your debt of gratitude. *You owe them—ALL of them—a huge Dream Debt!*

## How Do Your Repay Your Dream Debt?

You know, it amazes me that so many people today bury their dreams under a pile of half-baked excuses while dozens of dreams dangle just out of reach of their finger tips. They're like the fox in Aesop's fable, *The Fox and the Grapes*. The fox can't quite reach the grapes, so he quits trying, rationalizing "I didn't really want those grapes, anyway!" Today, millions of Dream Fakers and Undertakers are giving up trying to reach their dreams, rationalizing that they didn't really want those dreams anyway!

*Well, I say you can't give up on your dreams because you have a Dream Debt to pay!*

Somewhere in your past, you owe a debt of gratitude to the hundreds of courageous ancestors who scrimped and saved... hustled and labored... fought and survived... so that their descendants—YOU—could have a better opportunity to live your dreams.

Our ancestors left hopeless situations in other lands so that YOU could have a better life. They endured grinding, dirt-poor-paying jobs so that YOU could earn more for yourself and your family. They fled religious persecution in their birth land so that YOU could worship God as you choose.

How do you repay a Dream Debt? There's only one way to repay a dream debt—*you have to make an all-out effort to live your dreams!* That's it—that's the only way to repay your Dream Debt to all the people who suffered and sacrificed so that YOU could *have more* and *be more*. And the only way to truly *have more* and *be more* is to pursue your dreams with passion and purpose. Anything short of that, and you're defaulting on your Dream Debt.

Yes, you owe it to yourself to become a Dream Maker in a dream-taking world. But most of all, you owe it to the thousands of people who sacrificed *most* of their dreams… so that you could live *all* of yours.

STRATEGY **10**

# Act As If the Biggest Room Is the Room for Improvement

*There's only one corner of the universe you can be certain of improving, and that's your own self.*

–Aldous Huxley,
British author

Here's a true story that sounds like something out of *Ripley's Believe It or Not!*

One of the best-known, best-loved broadcasters in the world was once forbidden by a network president to ever appear on camera again because he hated her "high-pitched, squeaky voice." Years later, believe it or not, the same broadcaster *signed a contract with NBC for $65 million for five years!*

So, who was this squeaky-voiced TV personality who rose from the ashes of humiliation to the highest echelon of broadcasting? None other than Katie Couric, veteran co-host of NBC's *Today Show* and the highest paid woman on network TV.

Now, imagine for a moment that you're standing in Katie Couric's shoes when you get the news that the president of the network *forbids* you to appear in front of a camera again.

Think about it—this wasn't some addle-brained boss who's trying to squash your dream. **THIS WAS THE HEAD OF A MULTI-BILLION-DOLLAR MEDIA COMPANY TELLING YOU AND ALL YOUR CO-WORKERS THAT YOU'RE A DISGRACE TO TELEVISION!** How would you feel? Totally devastated, right? What would you do? Probably resign on the spot and start looking into other careers.

But not Katie Couric. She looked herself in the mirror and decided that the criticism was brutal but accurate. Instead of choosing to get a different dream, Couric chose to get better at her craft. So she hired a speech coach and continued her dream of becoming a newscaster.

## From Zero to Hero

Wow!—talk about belief in yourself! Talk about determination! Talk about overcoming obstacles to live your dream! Couric was driven by a lifelong dream of becoming an on-air investigative reporter, so she picked herself up and did what she had to do to live her dream. As a result, she's been the cornerstone of NBC's very popular and very profitable morning program for nearly a decade and is being groomed as "the next Barbara Walters."

Katie Couric became a Dream Maker because she exemplifies *Strategy #10: Act As If the Biggest Room Is the Room for Improvement.* You see, Couric had every excuse to abandon her dream. After all, she was publicly criticized by one of the most powerful men in television. How many people would continue climbing toward their dream after receiving that kind of criticism?

But Couric was a winner, not a quitter, and she kept true to her dream by maintaining a positive attitude and improving her craft. Couric wasn't handed her $12 million-a-year contract because she was blessed with a great voice for broadcasting. Or because she was in the right place at the right time. Or because she got all the breaks. She *earned* her multi-million-dollar-a-year salary by working on her weaknesses. Katie Couric became a Dream Maker because she literally improved her way to the top!

## Give Yourself a Chance by Getting Better

Sadly, for every Katie Couric, there are a thousand people who fold their tents and allow someone else to determine their dreams. So sad—and so unnecessary! Unlike royalty, Dream Makers don't inherit their dreams. Dream Makers have to earn their dreams by working hard *on their dreams*... while working just as hard *on themselves.* Dream Fakers and Undertakers think that personal growth is a waste of time. Dream Makers, on the other hand, understand that if you're not working on yourself, you're just not working. As the CEO of a Fortune 500 company observed, "The hardest thing about climbing the ladder of success is getting through the crowd at the bottom." Dream Makers understand that personal growth is the key to standing above the crowd and moving up the ladder.

You know, there's a word for the crowd of Dream Fakers and Undertakers gathered at the bottom of the ladder of success. That word is *mediocrity.* Here's my definition of mediocrity: "Mediocrity is the best of the worst and the worst of the best." Dream Makers aren't interested in accepting mediocrity—"the best of the worst." Dream Makers are only interested in achieving *excellence—the best of the best!* That's why Dream Makers dedicate themselves to lifelong learning and personal growth. Dream Makers understand that you can't become what you need to become if you remain what you are.

## Power of Reading

There are lots of ways to get information that will "furnish" your room for improvement, but, being a former English teacher and now a writer, the medium I'm most partial to is reading. Yes, you can get basically the same information watching a good movie version of *Huckleberry Finn* as you can reading Twain's classic novel. But there's somcthing about the act of reading that makes it superior to listening or watching.

Reading has been defined as "visually guided thinking," an apt description, for the act of reading forces us to think deeper and harder than when we just watch or listen.

When we read, we're forced to use our imagination to create and re-create the text. Which is why reading requires more active participation than TV watching.

Just think of all of the mental gymnastics we go through when we read: We translate the printed symbols into spoken words. We process the information. We paint mental pictures. We challenge the concepts. We criticize... attack... accept... defend... sympathize... laugh... memorize... repeat... review... absorb... ponder... scan... document... compare... and reject the information we read, all in the course of reading a text.

Considering the life-enhancing power of reading, you'd think that people would read every chance they get. Sadly, that's not the case. According to government statistics, TV now takes up 40% of the average American's free time. Americans spend 4.4 hours a day watching TV but only 17 minutes a day reading books. Imagine what would happen if this statistic were reversed and people read 4.4 hours a day—you'd have a lot more people climbing the ladder of success and a lot fewer standing at the bottom, wouldn't you agree?

## Why Soft Skills Form Rock-Hard Foundations

When I was teaching high school, my students would often complain about the reading assignments I gave them. Typically, the complaints would go something like, "Why do we have to read this story? I'm going to be a hair stylist. How will this stupid story help me cut hair?"

At the time, I didn't have a very good answer to that question. And it deserves a good answer. Think about it—if you're an accountant, it's obvious that the more accounting classes and seminars you attend, the better you'll be at your craft. Let's call these job-specific skills "hard skills." It's pretty obvious that you want your accountant or attorney or auto mechanic to have mastered the hard skills of their craft.

But why should accountants (or hair stylists, for that matter) waste their time learning "soft skills" (also known as "life skills" or "people skills")? Why should accountants read plays by Shakespeare? Why should attorneys listen to audio tapes on attitude? Why should auto mechanics attend seminars on relationship building? Why should dentists watch videos about leadership?

The best way to answer these questions is to tell you about the migration habits of a tiny bird called the swallow. Most likely you're heard of the famous "swallows of Capistrano." Every year the swallows fly 6,000 miles from Buenos Aires, Argentina, to San Juan Capistrano, a small town in southern California.

> I don't design clothes. I design Dreams.
>
> –Ralph Lauren, fashion designer

Amazingly, most of the migration is over open ocean. For years nobody could figure out how these tiny birds made such a long trip. Swallows can't swim. They can't fly 6,000 miles non-stop. So how did they complete their migration?

Researchers discovered that the swallows carry a twig in their beaks during migration, a big burden for such small birds on a long journey. When the swallows get tired, they drop their twigs in the water and float on them until they're rested. Then they resume their flight until they reach their destination.

Like swallows, people are on a long, arduous migration, too. Our migration is called life. Soft skills are to people what twigs are to swallows—a life raft in an ocean of constant change. If all you have to fall back on is your hard skills, you're going to sink. If you made your living repairing digital pagers, for example, what good will your job-specific hard skills do you when cell phones replace pagers? But if you have good soft skills, you can easily transition to a different career.

Soft skills are portable from one career to another, from one situation to another, from one role to another, from one life passage to another. Soft skills help you at home, as well as on the job. Soft skills last a lifetime, so they never become outdated or obsolete. And, more often than not, soft skills are what distinguish the exceptional people climbing the ladder of success... from the mediocre people standing at the bottom.

## You Can't Major in "Presidenting"

To prove my point that soft skills are essential for success, just look at the job description for the most powerful position in the world: president of the United States. What hard skills are necessary for the president's job? Virtually none. I mean, how does somebody train to be president of the United States? You can't enroll in "Running the Country 101," can you? How about acing a course called, "Putting Out Fires in the Middle East"? There's no such animal, is there?

The skills necessary to become an effective president are the same skills necessary to be an effective business person or an effective parent: Good leadership skills. Good communication skills. Good listening skills. Good problem-solving skills. Good sales skills. Good organizing skills. Good time-management skills. And on and on.

Yes, it goes without saying that a big part of furnishing your room for improvement is learning and mastering the job-specific hard skills of your chosen profession. But,when all is said and done, it's the soft skills that will enable you to become a Dream Maker in a dream-taking world.

## Personal Growth: Home Schooling Yourself

Because we're on the topic of presidents (and because I'm a former teacher), I can't resist giving you a pop quiz. Here's a question right out of your high school history book:

**Question:** *Who is the only U.S. president in the 20th century not to have a college degree?*

**Answer:** *Harry Truman, the 33rd president of the United States.*

Now, notice I didn't ask, "Who was the least educated president?" And for good reason. Truth is, Truman may have had the *least formal education,* but some historians would argue that he was the *most educated president* of the last 100 years, including Woodrow Wilson, a former president of Princeton University.

Huh?—how could a high school graduate like Truman be better educated than a college president? Because Truman was a voracious reader and an apt student all of his life. He read the Bible from cover to cover twice before the age of 12. After reading all of the history books in his hometown library, he reportedly read the *Encyclopedia Britannica* from A to Z. During his lifetime, Truman read and re-read the collected works of Shakespeare, Mark Twain, and Charles Dickens, plus thousands of history books and biographies of famous people.

Although Truman was a bookworm, he also understood that mentors were an invaluable source of learning and personal growth. When he was first elected to the U.S. Senate, for example, Truman made it a point to socialize with politicians from both parties. He scheduled breakfast, lunch, and dinner—as well as after-hour poker games—with Washington insiders, educating himself by listening to their stories, asking questions, provoking discussions, and then recording his new-found wisdom in long letters to his wife and nightly writings in his diaries.

> You look at any giant corporation, and I mean the biggies, and they all started with a guy with a dream, doing it well.
>
> –Irv Robbins,
> co-founder, Baskin-Robbins Ice Cream

David McCullough, the author of a critically acclaimed 1,000-page biography on Truman, once asked Truman's daughter, Margaret, what she thought her father's idea of heaven would be.

"Oh, that's easy," she replied. "It would be a good comfortable armchair and a good reading lamp and a stack of newly published histories and biographies that he wanted to read."

Harry Truman was living proof that the best way to get through the crowd at the bottom of the ladder of success is to keep learning and growing and improving in all phases of your life. How do you do that? Through purposeful, self-directed education and training, that's how.

I call it "home schooling yourself," and it's the only way to grow yourself to your fullest potential. It's no coincidence that two of our least formally educated presidents, Harry Truman and Abraham Lincoln, grew to become two of history's most respected leaders. They were both Dream Makers from humble backgrounds who rose to the exalted position of U.S. president by acting as if the biggest room is the room for improvement.

## How Do You Home School Yourself?

So, how do home school yourself—what "courses" do you take and how do you get the knowledge and wisdom that will grow you to your fullest potential? You have to do what Dream Makers like Harry Truman and Katie Couric did—identify your weaknesses and then get the education and training that will strengthen those weaknesses. In other words, successful home schoolers know what they don't know, then they go get it!

Home schooling yourself is like going to high school or college except you're responsible for designing your own curriculum. True, you may ask a trusted, knowledgeable advisor to help you design your course of study. But in the end, you're responsible for home schooling yourself. You choose the course content. You choose the reading material. You choose the videos to watch and the audios to listen to. You choose the live lectures and seminars to attend. You choose the "professors" and experts to mentor you, as well as the "fellow students" you want to hang out with between classes.

Why are books, tapes, and live lectures essential to your personal growth? The best way to answer that is with a quote by legendary photographer of the American West, Ansel Adams:

*You don't make a photograph just with a camera.*
*You bring to the act of photography all the pictures*
*you have seen, the books you have read, the music*
*you have heard, the people you have loved.*

What Adams is saying is that people, not cameras, take photographs. It follows, then, that the more well-informed and well-rounded a person becomes, the better they'll be at their chosen profession.

That's why NBA coach Phil Jackson hand-picks books for his players to read and discuss with him on long plane flights between games. Jackson understands that basketball players aren't wind-up toys—they're human beings who just happen to have a talent for playing a childhood game. Grow the person, Jackson reasons, and you grow the basketball player, too.

Does Jackson's unconventional strategy work? Considering that Jackson has the highest winning percentage of any coach in NBA history and has led his teams to eight NBA championships in his last 11 seasons, I think you'd have to agree that home schooling the whole person works wonders for basketball players—*and it can work wonders for you!*

# CONCLUSION

*People are never more insecure than when they become obsessed with their failures at the expense of their dreams*

–Norman Cousins,
writer

CONCLUSION

# If Dreams Were for Sale, What Would You Buy?

*Dream as if you'll live forever.*

–James Dean,
legendary actor

"H*ello. My name is Ernie Price, and I'm an alcoholic."*

I squirmed in my seat as I listened to my father's words. We were sitting in a damp, cold church basement in Champaign, Illinois, in the middle of winter, attending an Alcoholics Anonymous meeting. Outside, snow flakes fell as quietly as family secrets. Someone coughed. The heater kicked back on as my father continued.

*"I didn't drink because I loved being drunk. I drank because I hated being sober."*

I've reflected on these words hundreds of times over the last 25 years. I've come to realize that they're the key to unlocking the safe that contains my understanding of my father, Ernie Price, and his 50-year addiction to alcohol.

Until that evening, I'd always looked down on my father somewhat. Dismissed him as, well, weak. He'd embarrassed me in front of my friends dozens of times with his drinking. Humiliated me, even. One afternoon while playing golf with my two best college buddies, my father, drunk as usual, stumbled and fell down after shanking his drive 20 feet. Another time, he sang Hank Williams songs and told corny jokes to my high school basketball teammates who'd dropped by to drive me to a big game.

I don't remember if we won or lost that night.

I do remember that I didn't play very well.

I can't say I ever pitied my father. Certainly I never hated him. I hated his drinking and the ensuing humiliations. But not him. For the first 25 years of my life, I thought of my father like a coach thinks of the player who barely made the team—I sat him at the end of my emotional bench, talking to him only when I had to.

That all changed on the Tuesday night in a church basement in the middle of the frozen Illinois prairie when my father spoke the words, *"I didn't drink because I loved being drunk. I drank because I hated being sober."*

I was 25 when I heard those words. My father was in his 60s. His words warmed my frozen heart. I could feel 20-year-old walls of resentment melting like a child's snow fort in the April sun. Finally, I understood why my father drank.

My father didn't drink because he wanted to hurt me.

My father drank because he hurt.

## Healing the Hurts

As my heart thawed, our relationship began to heal. Like most men, my father had trouble expressing his feelings. I never heard my father say, "I love you," although he showed his love in hundreds of ways. Inviting me to attend an AA meeting was his way of saying, "I recognize I did some things to hurt you, and I'm sorry."

I'm happy to report that by the time I reached my early 30s, we became very close. My father's drinking days were behind him, and I finally grew up and forgave him for having faults. My father was a wonderful man. Funny. Patient. Tender-hearted. I don't ever remember his criticizing anything I did (although over the years, I did my share of knuckle-headed things that warranted criticism).

Every Christmas and Father's Day, I wrote my father a letter telling him how much I loved him and what made him so special to me. He never mentioned the letters to me. Never thanked me. I understood. Men of his generation born and raised in coal mining country just didn't say mushy things to their sons. But my mom told me Dad would sit in his favorite chair and read my letters over and over. Then she whispered, "And sometimes he cries."

Eighteen years after my father's last drink of alcohol, as he lay dying in a nursing home, he finally found the courage to say the words that he'd buried under a pile of unspoken feelings.

"Steve, I'm sorry if I hurt you with my drinking."

"Dad, no need to apologize. You never hurt me."

But we both knew otherwise.

We both knew that living with an alcoholic is like getting a smallpox vaccination—it leaves a small outward scar on us survivors, but inside, we build up emotional immunities to protect ourselves. Problem is, the scar fades, but the immunities endure. And as adults, sometimes we can't figure out which feelings we're immune to.

## Winning Against the Odds

Hundreds of people attended my father's funeral in 1993. I sat in the front row holding my mother's hand as my best friend read the eulogy I wrote. After the service, a man in his 40s introduced himself.

"I attended AA meetings with your dad," he said. "I always enjoyed listening when he talked—he always had something interesting to say."

"Thank you," I said. "He was a very wise man."

"By the way," the man continued. "Your father remained sober the rest of his life, didn't he?"

"Yes," I said proudly. "He remained drink-free for the last 18 years of his life."

"That's what I thought," the man said quietly. "Would you happen to know what percentage of alcoholics in recovery remain sober for the rest of their lives?"

"No," I replied.

"Two percent, at the most" he replied. "Two percent of the people who stop drinking never take another drink. Two percent, tops. Your dad was a pretty special man."

Suddenly, the sun burned off the gray fog shrouding my judgment, revealing a wonderful, technicolor truth: Only two percent of alcoholics—*that's two out of 100 people!*—remain sober for the rest of their lives. And Ernie Price, my dad, was one of those!!

## My Father, My Hero

Prior to that conversation, I'd never thought of my father as a Dream Maker. I thought all my dad ever dreamed of was a secure job, even if it were a job he grew to hate.

But as I look back on my father's life, I realize he used many of the Dream Making strategies in this book to free himself from alcoholism. He stopped shopping for excuses. He traveled on the train tracks by attending AA. He was an all-out, not a hold-out. He pushed the envelope of his expectations. And he continued to improve as a person, father, and husband until he died in his 80s.

In a sense, my father was more than just a Dream Maker. He was the Ultimate Dream Maker, for his dream transcended fancy houses and foreign cars. *His dream was to be free*—and he made that dream come true!

He lived his dream of being free from addiction to alcohol.

He lived his dream of being free from self-contempt.

He lived his dream of being free to look his wife and two sons in the eyes and say, "I battled addiction. And I won!"

You see, my father understood that dreams are for sale, but they all have a price tag. My father, thank God, was willing to pay the price to live his dreams. He paid the price by being painfully honest with himself and his family. By remaining strong in the face of temptation. And by attending AA meetings five nights a week for 15 years, eventually scaling back to twice a week the last three years of his life.

To me, Ernie Price was more than a Dream Maker in a dream-taking world.

*Ernie Price, my father, was my hero!*

## What About You?

What about you?

What are your dreams?

If dreams were for sale, what would *you* buy?

Are you willing to pay the price to live those dreams?

If you look deep inside, you'll recognize that, like my father, you, too, have a big dream. You can ignore it. You can deny it. You can even bury it. But in your quiet moments, you bring it out, dust it off, and stare at it longingly.

Well, wouldn't you agree that it's time you stopped shopping for excuses and started becoming a Dream Maker?

If my father can kick a 50-year addiction to alcohol and live his dream of freedom, you can live your dream.

If the dozens of people profiled in this book can overcome obstacles and live their dreams, you can live your dreams.

So go ahead—dare to dream. And then dare to do what it takes to live your dream. Then one day, like me, your children will be able to say:

*"My Dad... and my Mom, are my heroes!"*